BAYNARD RUSH HALL:
HIS STORY
by DIXIE KLINE RICHARDSON

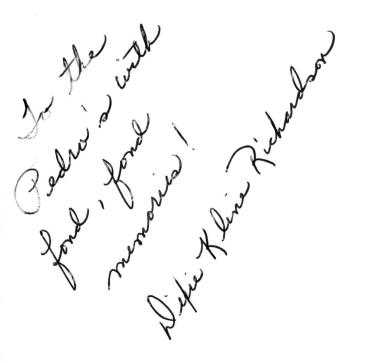

To the Pedro's, with fond, fond memories!

Dixie Kline Richardson

Printed in the United States of America

Library of Congress Cataloging-in-Publication Data
Richardson, Dixie Kline
Baynard Rush Hall: His Story
by Dixie Kline Richardson

ISBN 978-0-615-36316-5

Table of Contents

Preface

Baynard Rush Hall (1798–1863) born in Philadelphia; Presbyterian pastor, author and educator. First instructor at Indiana Seminary. Principal of private boarding schools. Lecturer. "Said to be entertaining."

Pardon my bias. I've been in love with Baynard Rush Hall since the day I accidentally jostled his first book off a library shelf and it fell into my hands. That was over 35 years ago. it is not my intention to rewrite his *The New Purchase*: or, *Seven and a Half Years in the Far West* and his revision of it, but to set the record straight. The book and the man have been misunderstood, misjudged, and misread. I have wanted to restore interest in both, whether my book is read as a prequel or sequel to his work. Like the author, I may be attacked for what I left out and what I put in. If accused of sentimentality and provincialism, no contest.

It is my intent to identify people, places, and events, and especially to bring some order of time to *The New Purchase*...as well as to tell the entire story of Baynard Rush Hall's life.

It is not possible to explain this complex and complicated man; that will be left to those who attempt to analyze from a distance. There is a goldmine to examine, explore, appraise, and expound. With a reasonable degree of certainty, I think he may have struggled with a bipolar illness. But at his best, he was a remarkable observer of human nature, the natural world around him, and the character of the time, people, and places he knew. He wrote with a wordsmith's pen. Sometimes he is more whimsical than methodical. He could be snarky and coy; he was witty and ethereal.

When *The New Purchase* is described as fiction, or a bitter diatribe, or ridicule, then the readers have not discerned that the book is storytelling, reminiscing as one would sit down with grandchildren and say, as Hoosiers do, "Well... once upon a time when I was little...." They do not get the affectionate satire, or catch that despite his sometimes hard edges, one can feel his good heart.

He has been and can be a subject for scholars of early travel, regional speech, slavery issues and social issues, education, religion, anti-intellectualism, gun laws, environmental studies, humor, customs, traditions, and even food preparation. But the worst sting is when his veracity is doubted. I heard playwright Harold Pinter remark in an interview that "in a work of art, there can be both true and false." There is truth in the belief that the truth is often more "unbelievable" than fiction. *The New Purchase* is primary source history; as the comedians say, "You can't make this stuff up." That his work is a true account of his time is recognized by those who know—more than a century after its publication. Author Meredith Nicholson said, "It has the flavor of sassafras, the soul lifting bouquet of the pawpaw. Sound Hoosier stuff. American stuff. It is a book of value. A work of charm, and whenever I pass it on the shelf, I bow to it as to something particularly worthy of honor."

Hall deliberately scrambled time, used pseudonyms that can't be, by rhyme or reason, translated into correct identities. Some of his characters have two fabricated names. It had to be hard work to make this fascinating book confusing. Yes, he was avoiding libel; but his devices wouldn't have gotten him off the hook. And yes, he admits literary license. Many of his detractors based their opinions on their impressions never having looked beyond his time in Bloomington, Indiana and the college years. They did not look at his life before Indiana or after. Richard Banta, author and historian, called him a "smart aleck;" Banta, who might have reveled in all of Baynard Hall's lifetime connections had he known about them, cried "snobbery."

Hall's other work, *Teaching a Science: Teacher as Artist*, is fodder for educators who examine methods past and present. Education and educators are always in a state of change in methods and philosophies. Hall had some very modern ideas, some that are quaint and literally "old school," but all make intriguing reading. Much of what he wrote about teaching and learning is surprisingly fresh and his theories are worth discussing.

Frank Freeman's Barber Shop is out there in cyberspace along with abolitionist, anti-abolitionist issues, and race related discussions. Before he is judged for not taking a more rigid anti-slavery stance, read the book and understand his life. He was a man with a foot in both worlds. In his day he associated with slave owners, and in Indiana and Philadelphia with former slave holders. Above all, his concern was the humane treatment of fellow human beings and this reflected the policy of many of the clergy who struggled with the ambiguities and complexities of this tragic problem.

Something for Every Body: Gleaned In The Old Purchase, From Fields Often Reaped covers his opinions and observations on topics of the time and is a study in insight. Here he reveals more of his pastoring nature and his Christian beliefs and biases. He also discloses more autobiographical material and all through what Shakespeare would describe as a "dialogue with thy shadow," in assuming the two characters who exchange correspondence.

In the six years I have worked toward the end of this biography, I have sometimes used my personal interpretation of what might be, just as W.E. Woodward said in his *George Washington:*

The Image and the Man (1926), "there is a strain of shrewdness in history-writing, as there is in law and business." I have pursued Baynard Hall from the alleys of Philadelphia to farmland in Indiana, rolling hills in Kentucky, a muddy road in South Carolina, to a lovely, quiet street in Brooklyn and a peaceful cemetery from which can be seen the skyscrapers of Manhattan. Maybe I know him as well as he can be known. I hope I have done him justice. I have researched institutions, libraries, courthouses, the internet, and have bought from rare book dealers all of his books. I have tracked what speeches could be found. I have tried to correctly identify the people he disguised and to detail with accuracy the extended family he loved. My husband and I read the 1843 edition of *The New Purchase* against the 1855 edition to record what revisions had been made. I translated, by hunting through lots of sources, all the Latin phrases and references from Shakespeare, Virgil and Horace which pepper his works. We slept in the house where he died.

He left some "keys" to his *New Purchase,* but he didn't tell all. It was the prankster in him. In the preface to the 1855 edition, he wrote, "In time, perhaps, a Key may be *forged* for the Lock. It is hoped, however, none but Masters will ever get in, or *advanced* Students afflicted with *Cacoethes Scribendi;* as such only will understand how out-of-the-way matters can be turned to a good account, and how a Man may use a liberty without abusing it." In the 1843 preface:

Let the book pass for what it is worth; if taken for History, it will be thought I had a somewhat remarkable experience, if for Fiction, that I have tolerable invention; and then my skull will be in the market--for the booksellers in my lifetime--and the Phrenologists afterwards. And yet, on second thought, you may say, that had I not told, sometimes less than the truth, the undiminished Truth would have seemed more like fiction than ever.

Dixie Kline Richardson
Indianapolis, Indiana
April 2009

Acknowledgement

My sincere gratitude to Priscilla Normandy Greenwood, Craig Kline, and Thom Richardson of our family for help and encouragement; to Deborah Millstein for inviting us into Hall's Brooklyn home; Donato Daddario, historian of the Cemetery of the Evergreens for the renovation of the Hall plot; Karen Kotlarchik of the Holmes family; Krys Douglas, Reed descendant; Sue Trotman, Gosport historian; Bridget Edwards, curator of education for the Wylie House, Bloomington; Brad Cook of Indiana University Archives, and my partner, Bart Richardson, who was there every step of the way.

Chronology

1745 Dr. Benjamin Rush born, December 24.

1753 Elizabeth Grimball marries William
      Baynard, February 1, have daughter
      Elizabeth Ann, birth date unknown.

1755 John Hall born, date unknown.

1762 Ann Holmes born, August 27.

1764 John Holmes born.

1773 Martha Holmes born.

1774 First Continental Congress meets,
      September 5.

1775 Battle of Bunker (Breed's) Hill.
      George III declares Colonies in rebellion.

1776 Congress adopts Jefferson's revised
      Declaration of Independence, July 4.

1777 British occupy Philadelphia, September 26
      to June, 1778.

1783 Formal end of the American Revolution,
      Treaty at Paris, September 3.

1787 Isaac Reed born, August 27.
      Constitution framed in Philadelphia, May
      to September.
      Dr. Rush assists newly founded Free
      African Society.

1788 Dr. John Hall and Elizabeth Baynard marry.

1789 U.S. Constitution ratified in Philadelphia. George Washington sworn in, New York, April 30.

1790 U.S. Capital moved from New York to Philadelphia. Washingtons move to Philadelphia, November.

1791 Bill of Rights becomes law, December 15.

1793 Yellow Fever in Philadelphia, begins mid-August.

Fifty-nine members of Second Presbyterian Church die, September.

Washington begins second term.

Martha Holmes marries Robert Doughty, Jr. May 17.

Dolley Payne Todd's husband John and youngest son die of Yellow Fever. (She marries James Madison.)

Ann Holmes living with sister Martha and Robert Doughty.

1795 Ann Holmes marries Nicholas Young, Jr., April 23.

1796 Mary Ann Young born, January 27.

Washington's "Farewell" in *American Daily Advertiser*, Philadelphia, September 19.

1797 Yellow Fever in Philadelphia, summer and fall.

John Morris Young born, September 2.

1798   Baynard Rush Hall born, January 28.
        Yellow Fever in Philadelphia, summer and fall.

1799   Elinor Young born, September 22.
        George Washington dies, December 14.

1800   Dr. John Hall signs his Will, September 21.

1801   Dr. John Hall signs codicil to Will, January 25.
        Dr. Rush writes in journal, death of his cousin, Dr. John Hall, January 25.

1802   Martha Washington dies, May 22.

1803   Martha Morris Young born, January 27.

1809   James Madison inaugurated President, March 4.

1811   Battle of Tippecanoe, Indiana Territory, November 7.

1812   President James Madison declares war with Great Britain, June 18.

1813   Dr. Benjamin Rush dies, April 19.

1814   British burn Washington, August 24, 25.
        Dolley Payne Todd Madison saves documents, and George Washington portrait.
        Treaty of Ghent signed to end war, December 24.

1815(ca) John Holmes goes to southern states;
        Thomas Holmes may have gone to Ohio.

1816 Indiana (bottom of) becomes 19th state, December 11.

Dr. David Maxwell pens the state's Constitution.

Group of notable, white males meets in Washington, D.C. to form a colonization society, December–January.

1817 Isaac Reed moves to Kentucky from Connecticut.

Abel Holmes, Jr., sibling of Ann, Martha, John, and Thomas, is in Kentucky.

1818 Martha Holmes Doughty (Aunt Doughty) is living with Abel Holmes, Jr. family in Kentucky.

Baynard Rush Hall is admitted to College of New Jersey, as a sophomore, May 12.

1819 Isaac Reed establishes Sunday School in New Albany, Indiana.

Baynard Hall requests dismissal from College of New Jersey, May 12.

Isaac Reed marries "in the evening" Elinor Young, in Danville, Kentucky, December 25.

Reed writes that Hall made a trip to the south in the winter of 1819.

1820 Indiana Legislature agrees to a state seminary, January 20.

Col. Williamson Dunn becomes registrar of Terre Haute, Indiana, District Land Office.

Rev. J.M. Dickey starts Bethany Church in Owen County, 22nd Presbyterian in Indiana, March 20.

Baynard Hall marries Mary Ann Young in Danville, Kentucky in May, day unknown.

Baynard Hall receives Bachelor of Arts from Union College, New York, July.

Seminary location chosen by state legislature, July.

Martha Doughty Reed born to Isaac and Elinor, Danville, November 1.

1821 Daphne Peterson makes Will, January 29.

Halls' baby boy John is born, July.

John Holmes, Ann Young, Martha Doughty join Bethany Presbyterian, November 11; John M. Young joins December 20.

1822 Martha Doughty buys 80 acres in Owen County, Indiana, February 22.

Halls' baby girl born in Philadelphia, June or July.

Ann Young Reed, born March 15, dies in Kentucky, August 28, day after father's birthday.

Isaac Reed and family leave Kentucky for Owen County, September 25; arrive first week in October.

Isaac Reed and Ann Young buy 80 acres; Isaac buys additional 80 acres, at Terre Haute Land Office; John Young accompanies Isaac on 50-mile trip, November 13.

1823   Lydia Ann Lapsley Reed born, May 25.

Big Fire dies, is buried in Owen County; Hunting Shirt Andy incident occurs, likely summer or fall.

Daphne Peterson dies, July 20.

Baynard Hall receives three-year certificate from Princeton Theological Seminary, September.

Baynard Hall licensed to preach, Philadelphia Presbytery, in Frankford, Pennsylvania, October.

Baynard Hall hired by Indiana Legislature, November? or some say year is 1824.

1824   Burial records of Second Presbyterian Church, Philadelphia, deaths of Hall children; son John Hall buried January 19; daughter buried January 30, Arch Street Cemetery.

First meeting of Salem Presbytery, April.

Ann Young buys 80 acres, April 15.

Baynard and Mary Ann Hall leave Philadelphia for Indiana, April.

Halls arrive in Young settlement, May.

Halls have baby daughter Elizabeth, date unknown.

Alternate possible date for Hall being hired as seminary instructor, November 24.

1825   Board of Trustees begins advertising the
        opening of Indiana Seminary.
        Hall, Bush, and Reed form Wabash
        Presbytery.
        Seminary begins, April 4, according to
        advertisements.
        Baynard Hall ordained by Isaac Reed, April
        13.
        Sarah Lewis Reed born to Isaac and Elinor,
        June 1.
        Presbytery annual meeting, Vincennes,
        Indiana, August 5; Hall hired as missionary
        for six weeks.

1826   Ann Young and Martha Doughty sell 80
        acres each, January 19; Ann moves in with
        Reeds in March.
        Seminary Trustees announced "second
        year" to begin May 1.
        Ann Young dies, April 5.
        Isaac Reed family leaves for New York,
        May 26.
        Thomas Holmes leaves Owen County.
        Thomas Jefferson, John Adams die, July 4.
        Baynard Hall and John Holmes attend
        synod at Vincennes, October.
        Baynard Hall preaches sermon in Indiana
        House of Representatives, December 31.
        Mary Ann Hall and sister Martha Young
          advertise Young Ladies Institute, Bloomington.

1827 John Hopkins Harney hired to teach at seminary.

George Whitefield Reed born in New York, June 25.

Baynard Hall receives honorary master's degree, Miami University.

1828 Indiana Seminary becomes a college, January 24. Baynard Hall named professor of ancient languages.

John M. Young, state representative.

Baynard Hall writes in May that he has buried an infant daughter (birth, death date, name unknown).

The Guzzleton (Gosport) Barbecue, actual year not determined.

Rush Baynard Hall born.

Isaac Reed's *The Christian Traveler* published.

1829 Elinor Catherine Reed born, January 18.

John Young sells land containing mother Ann's grave, February 11.

John Young marries Aletha Wallace, May 6.

Town of Gosport platted, June 29.

Andrew Wylie, D.D. assumes duties as Indiana College President, October 29.

James Borland transfers seminary plot 38 in Bloomington to Halls and Martha Doughty, November 10.

1830 Isaac Reed family living next to Dr. David Maxwell.

First IU College class graduates.

Baynard Chisholm Hall born in May.

Henodelphisterian Society splits.

1831 John Young's son Wallace H. born in Gosport, February 23.

Baynard Hall finds anonymous letter.

First college catalog published.

Reeds conduct school in Bloomington.

College spring exhibition, May/June?

Chalmers Reed born, June 22.

Halls sell part of lot 38, May 24.

Alexis de Tocqueville ends tour of United States.

Baynard Hall resigns, but will stay a year, September 29.

1832 Holmes Baynard Hall born, February 14.

Elizabeth Hall, age eight, dies, June 2.

John Hopkins Harney dismissed, September 25.

Halls sell part of lot 38 to Harney, September 28.

Baynard Hall quits two weeks before Fall Commencement.

Halls leave Bloomington, October.

Last Signer of the Declaration of Independence, Charles Carroll, dies,

November 14.

Halls arrive in Bedford, Pennsylvania.

1833   John Morris Young Jr., born.

Baynard Chisholm Hall, age three, dies in Bedford, Pennsylvania, October.

1834   Isaac and Elinor Reed advertise school for males, females, to open in Bloomington in November.

John M. Young admitted to Hanover (Indiana) Presbyterian Church, May.

1835   Reeds move to Hanover, Indiana.

John Holmes admitted to Hanover Presbyterian Church, November.

Baynard Hall goes to Philadelphia to publish his Latin grammar, winter.

1836   Edistina Morris Hall, born.

Exercises, Analytical and Synthetical, arranged for the New and Compendious Latin Grammar, by Baynard R. Hall, A.M. published, month unknown.

One John Young marries Elizabeth Eckles in Owen County, this later appears in Indiana Legislature history; this is not John M. Young.

1837   Economy fails; banks close. This depression lasts until 1843.

Andrew Jackson ends second term.

1838   Baynard Hall produces "Disciplined Youth

Necessary for the Duties of Middle Life and the Comfort of Old Age."

Carolina Baynard Hall born, March 25.

1839   Halls are in Bordentown, New Jersey.

Martha Doughty Reed dies in Terre Haute, Indiana, April 8.

Baynard Hall speaks to young women at Spring-Villa Seminary, August 29.

1841   President William Henry Harrison dies, after 32 days in office, April 4.

Halls are in Trenton, New Jersey.

Baynard Hall transfers John Hall's 1795 land grant, October 21.

1842   Baynard Hall serving Second Presbyterian, Trenton.

Baynard Hall receives honorary Master of Arts *addendum*, College of New Jersey.

Baynard Hall at Bartlett's Institute, Poughkeepsie, New York; start date unknown.

1843   John M. Young and wife Aletha separated.

The New Purchase...published, month unknown, using pseudonym Robert Carlton, Esq., D. Appleton & Co., New York and Philadelphia.

1844   Texas becomes U.S. Territory.

John M. Young and Aletha divorced, September.

John Holmes dies at Hanover, age 80, November.

1845   John Morris Young is elected as Hanover College trustee.

Baynard Hall at Dutchess Academy, Poughkeepsie, New York.

1846   *Something for Every Body...*, with pseudonym Robert Carlton, published by Appleton, New York and Philadelphia.

1847   Baynard Hall resigns from Dutchess Academy, March 10.

Baynard Hall becomes Principal of Newburgh Academy, Orange County, New York.

The "American" Liberians declare independence, July 26.

1848   Hall's *Teaching a Science: The Teacher as Artist* published by Baker and Scribner, New York.

Baynard Hall receives honorary Doctor of Divinity from Rutgers.

1850   Halls in Newburgh, New York with students boarding in their home.

1851   Stowe's *Uncle Tom's Cabin,* appearing in serial form.

1852   *Uncle Tom's Cabin* in book form, March.

Frank Freeman's Barber Shop, Scribner's first edition published, month unknown.

Baynard Rush Hall speaks at College of New Jersey, June 25.

Halls living in Brooklyn.

Baynard Hall pastoring Dutch Reformed Church.

1853   *Frank Freeman's Barber Shop*, second edition published by Alden, Wanzer, with Beardsley & Co. with an elaborate new cover.

1854   Rush Baynard Hall dies, March 12.

Dr. David H. Maxwell dies, May 24.

1855   *The New Purchase...*, revised edition, published by John Nunemacher, New Albany, Indiana.

Whitman's *Leaves of Grass* published.

1856   Henry Ward Beecher's slave auction sermons in Brooklyn.

"Know-Nothing" party evolves; Kansas-Nebraska Act foments slavery issues.

1857   U.S. Supreme Court declares blacks, slaves and free, non-citizens; and Congress cannot prohibit slavery in Dred Scott Decision, March.

Hall lectures at Rutgers Female Institute, December.

1858   Isaac Reed dies, January 14.

1859   Edistina M. Hall dies, May 24.

1861   First shot of Civil War at Fort Sumter, Charleston Harbor, South Carolina, April 12.

1862 George Whitefield Reed dies in battle, August 9.

Preliminary Emancipation Proclamation, September 22.

Baynard Hall ends pastorate at Dutch Reformed Church, Brooklyn.

1863 Emancipation Proclamation, January 1.

Baynard Rush Hall dies, January 23.

1864 Carolina Baynard Hall dies, February 2.

Martha Holmes Doughty (Aunt Doughty) dies, July 24.

Holmes Baynard Hall dies, September 29.

Mary Ann Young Hall dies, November 10.

1865 Lee surrenders at Appomattox, April 9.

Lincoln assassination, April 14.

1866 Martha Morris Young dies, November 14.

1867 John Hopkins Harney dies, January 27.

1869 Elinor Young Reed dies. May 9.

1870 John Morris Young, Sr., living in Missouri.

1873 Indiana State Teachers Association in *The Indiana School Journal* says Seminary opened in May 1825.

1906 Dr. John Hall's North Carolina property is involved in land transactions; Martha Morris Young's Will entered in Hyde County records.

1914   Martha Morris Young's Will appears in Hyde and Tyrrell counties, North Carolina records. Dr. John Hall's in Hyde County.

1916   *The New Purchase: or, Seven and a Half Years in the Far West,* by Robert Carlton, Esq. (aka: Baynard Rush Hall) 1843, republished by Princeton University Press, Indiana Centennial Edition edited by Indiana University professor Dr. James Albert Woodburn.

Indiana celebrates centennial year.

1975   Arno Press, in "Mid-America Frontier" series reprints original 1843 edition of *The New Purchase...*

Baynard Rush Hall
Family of Origin

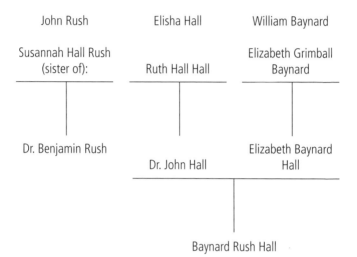

John Rush   Elisha Hall   William Baynard

Susannah Hall Rush
(sister of):   Ruth Hall Hall   Elizabeth Grimball
Baynard

Dr. Benjamin Rush

Dr. John Hall   Elizabeth Baynard
Hall

Baynard Rush Hall

The Young Settlement Family
and
Their Children

Thomas Holmes	Ann Holmes	John Holmes	Martha Holmes
Nancy	Nicholas Young, Jr.	Wife Unknown	Robert Doughty, Jr.

	Mary Ann Young	John Morris Young	Elinor Young	MARTHA MORRIS YOUNG
	Baynard Rush Hall	Aletha Wallace	Isaac Reed	

John Hall		Wallace H. Young	Martha Doughty Reed
daughter		John M. Young, Jr.	Ann Young Reed
Elizabeth Hall			Lydia Ann Lapsley Reed
daughter			Sarah Lewis Reed
Rush Baynard Hall			George Whitefield Reed
Baynard Chisholm Hall			Elinor Catherine Reed
Holmes Baynard Hall			Chalmers Reed
Edistina Morris Hall			
Carolina Baynard Hall			

Chapter 1

Tadpole state between child and boy.

"Snow about an inch deep. Clear and wind at Northwest. Mercury at 20 in the morning." As was his custom, George Washington, farmer and former President, recorded the weather at Mount Vernon in his diary on January 28, 1798. On that date in Philadelphia, Dr. John Hall, aging at 42, and his wife Elizabeth became parents of a son. It was a cold and bleak time for a confinement, and there may have been little hope for this baby because the Halls had lost a child every year of their marriage. He was given the name Baynard Rush, using his mother's maiden name and the surname of Dr. John Hall's first cousin, Dr. Benjamin Rush. The boy was born at Turner's Lane on the Delaware side of the neat rectangle laid out between two rivers and at a time when Philadelphia was second only to London as a cosmopolitan city and not yet a generation removed from the Revolution.

Three years later in January, Benjamin Rush, Signer of the Declaration of Independence, cohort, friend, advisor, and sometimes adversary of the notables of the Revolution, the Constitution, and four Presidents, entered into his journal:

> This day died my dear Cousin Dr. Jno. Hall. He left me his executor and guardian of his only son. His black woman, whom he had emancipated twenty years before, said he had been her master, father, and mother. If, said she, any man had taken him away, I would tear him to pieces, but as God Almighty has done it, why I must submit.

John Hall died three days short of his only child's third birthday according to Dr. Rush's journal, dating the death as January 25. Dr. Rush told no more about his cousin, but in later years Baynard Hall will state that his father was a surgeon in the Revolution. John Hall's older brother, Dr. Elisha Hall, consulted Dr. Rush in treating Washington's mother for breast cancer, and was, at least once, a guest at Mount Vernon. Doctors Elisha and John Hall were sons of Elisha and Ruth Hall. Ruth, a sister of Susannah Hall Rush, mother of Dr. Rush, did not have to change her monogram when she married.

John Hall wrote his own Will on September 21, 1800, just four months before his death at 45 and having had truck with lawyers, shrewdly stated:

> As this will was made just as I was

Leaving the City & without form notwithstanding, it expresses my intentions
I beg & request my Executors will as
nearly as possible act accordingly and
not be regulated by interference of Law
opinion or otherwise.

John Hall's practice of medicine in Philadelphia
may have been limited or perhaps set aside; it
appears that his avocation was speculation in land.
At the time he penned his Will, he was on his way
to Georgia where he had been involved either as an
agent for the purchase of large tracts working for
or with Wade Hampton, one of the South's record
landowners, and possibly Senator James Gunn, and
also as an individual investor. History labeled some
of this Georgia land grab the Yazoo Land Fraud.
Documents in 1793 suggest that Dr. Hall was either
buying or promoting the sale of Pine Barren lands
in what was another scandal; in that instance, the
doctor could have been a victim of fraudulent
sales.

In his Will he requested that his son be educated
and specified that "old Daphney" be his son's nurse
and be supported out of the estate. Calling her
one of his mothers, Baynard Hall wrote of Daphne
Peterson that she was "the dear old Negro woman
who nursed and loved me." Dated on the day of Dr.
Hall's death, a codicil with a shaky version of his
very distinctive signature, designates Richard Rush,
son of Dr. Rush, as an additional executor, as well
as Hall's brother Richard and John Hall, probably

a cousin. Attorney Peter Conway was already a co-executor with Dr. Rush. Why this codicil, dated on the day he died, adds three additional overseers is one of the several mysteries left by Dr. John Hall.

To his son, Dr. Hall bequeathed half his wearing apparel and one half of his deceased wife's clothes, the couple's gold watches, all the plate, proceeds of half of his British claim in the name of Ben M. Morgan, also a part of a tract of land in North Carolina containing 22,400 acres and a portion of all his Pennsylvania lands. Shares of these lands were also given to a boy named John Wyatt and a little girl he named as Harriatt Hawkins. Who these children are is a puzzle. The surnames do not appear among immediate relatives. Some of Mrs. Hall's clothing was to be given to Dr. Hall's niece, Elizabeth, a daughter of Richard. Attorney Peter Conway's wife was to be given a share of that clothing. It may be of no consequence, but Richard Hall and Peter Conway are listed in bankruptcy records between 1800–1806. Requesting Dr. Rush to take his three-year-old son "under his care and patronage," Hall asked Benjamin Rush to "educate him as he may think proper."

A sampling of the inventory of Dr. Hall's estate includes five gold watches, linens, lace, fabrics, assorted jewelry, six "pettycoats," "1 fine muslin dress," four silver table spoons, a pap spoon, portmanteau trunk and demijohn, holsters and pistols, a horseman's sword, bedding, a guitar, two new patched work bedspreads, three horses (at

$113.00 each), a phaeton and hames, a Bible and four books, and a portrait of George Washington. Women's clothing and jewelry indicate that Dr. Hall had not parted with his deceased wife's possessions. The small number of books, the sparseness of household furniture, a fairly meager amount of men's clothing, the fact that some items were situated in the house of another, and the absence of any residence, suggest the Halls had been living in a boarding house.

Dr. John Hall was the owner of a 1795 North Carolina land grant containing five tracts amounting to a total of 214,480 acres in then Hyde County. A subsequent deed in 1841 states that 14,160 acres had been granted out of the first tract leaving 195,840 acres in that tract. A suit to quiet title to these thousands of acres many years later makes the discovery that the land had been sold for taxes in 1801 when Dr. Hall died and when Baynard Hall was three years old. No taxes had ever been paid by the owner, representatives or heirs. Details of time, place, and agents of the 14,160-acre transfer are unknown.

My mother's family belonged to Edisto Island and to Georgia.

In late summer of 1798, Yellow Fever in Philadelphia kept Dr. Rush on his feet night and day and eventually killed 3,637 people. He described this outbreak as much more malignant than those of 1793 and 1797, which had struck the city like an Old Testament curse. The recurring malarial disease made onslaughts that lasted until a killing frost exterminated the mosquitoes that carried the infection. It is entirely possible that both Dr. John Hall and his wife were victims. When Elizabeth Ann Baynard Hall died is unknown; her death occurred sometime between May 1798 when she cosigned a land transaction with her husband, and his death in September 1801. During this epidemic, Dr. Rush sent his family out of the city, obsessed over the appearance of unfamiliar symptoms, and burned the midnight oil in search of cause and cure. While a number of Philadelphia physicians involved in the plague seasons are a matter of record, the name of a Dr. John Hall is absent. The practice of medicine did not guarantee a lucrative income and likely Dr. Hall was riding his horse through canebrake and marsh grass rather than making house calls.

Elizabeth Hall's people were South Carolina low-country, slave-owning planters whose livelihood came from the production of sea-island cotton, much of it exported to Europe for manufacture of finer grade fabric. On Edisto Island, Elizabeth's parents, William and Elizabeth Grimball Baynard, were landed gentry. Elizabeth Grimball married William Baynard in 1753; their children included sons Thomas and William, and daughter Elizabeth. Baynard Hall's maternal grandmother was a daughter of Paul Grimball with ancestry linked to the first Paul Grimball whose 1,590-acre land grant was recorded in 1683.

Baynard was aware of his mother's planter-culture aristocracy. He traveled to South Carolina and probably into Georgia at least twice not only to settle financial matters, but out of a need to connect with his maternal roots. With tongue in cheek, he wrote of the Baynards, "perhaps the name is Norman French, probably we are related to 'Baynard Castle' or some old feudal robber that built it." This connection to England is verified by future generations of Baynard genealogists. He does not indicate any specific references to his father's relatives.

Upon the death of John Hall, Dr. Rush, possibly the busiest man in Philadelphia, 56 years old, with his wife Julia raising their last four children (between 10 and infancy) is left with the burden of a three-year-old boy. In a letter in June, just after Rush's last child William had been born, Rush wrote, "An addition of a ninth living child (William) to my family a few weeks ago will protract my labors in Philadelphia for many years to come."

Hall's surviving maternal uncles in South Carolina, Thomas and William Baynard, were raising their own broods: Thomas with four boys under 10 and an older daughter; his brother William had four children under 10. Early on, Dr. Rush must have appealed to the uncles to take their little namesake back to his mother's home. A response from Thomas Baynard is dated November 9, 1801 just as Baynard is about to be four years of age; Dr. Rush has been his guardian for 10 months:

We are sorry so much time has been lost in our communications. Yours not coming to hand for four Months from the Date. Your kindness in Taking Care of our Nephew and Writing to us We gratefully acknowledge. Your reasons and Objections to your future care So just that it leaves us at a loss What to Say on the Business—it being our Sincere Desire to act for his Good was the reasons which induced us to continue him under your Guardianship. Not Immediately Considering he was to remain in Your Family as we tho't, you might have him Boarded out in a situation where you could have seen Justice done him Without any Disadvantage to yourself. The expense you mention for his Maintenance and Schooling We would chearfully [sic] pay. But my Dear Sir it is not Expence [sic] we look at but the benefit we hope our Nephew would receive from this consideration & this alone rises our Wish of keeping him to the Northward. Situated as we are on a Small Island with only one Schoolmaster & That one only an English Teacher which renders it impossible for us to give him that Chance his Genius Merits (under our eyes) & which we would by no means have to be dormant, Considering it our Duty to

have him Bro't up in the best Manner as
by his Abilities & Qualifications we must
Expect him to live should Providence
Spare him to pass Through the World in
Credit & Honor. We at present pay for
our Small Children Sixty-four Dollars a
Year for Schooling alone and are obliged
to put them out, also the School being
so far Distant from us. The Fever which
of late years has made such Havoc in
Chston the Only place Near us where it
is possible to get him Educated forbids a
Tho't of placing him There. What can we
father [*sic*] say. My Dear Sir After Stating
This facts we have only to add Should it
Appear Best to you & Agreeable to your
Wish as his Adopted Father to Commit
him to our Care our Harts [*sic*] are open
and ready for his reception. Should you
think proper to keep him we shall be ready
to pay your Draughts at Sight & are very
willing should it be necessary to Enhance
his Maintenance/Schooling &C to Three
Hundred Dollars. On the contrary Should
you Determine on Sending him to us You
will Commit him to the Care of Messrs.
Miller & Robertson of Charleston & in
future Direct my letters to their Care.

With the Greatest Esteem. We are
Dr. Sir Yr Mot Obdt Servants Thomas &
William Baynard

There is some sense of push–pull in what can be read between the lines of the Baynard brothers' response to Dr. Rush, and in spite of their genteel "greatest esteem" for Rush, there is a coolness emanating from this letter. Nothing has been uncovered that suggests Dr. Hall's survivors were asked to care for the child. Is it possible that at a tender age this boy intuited that people in his life had abandoned or rejected him.

Dr. Rush's response was the request that $250.00 be sent "punctual and annually," and in return he would send an account of expenditures. Dr. Rush's memorandum book shows receipts from Thomas Baynard from December 1802 through June 1807 in various amounts from an initial $250.00 to $47.50. In November 1802, Thomas Baynard wrote that his brother William had died five months earlier. Receipts to Baynard's account then appear to come from agents. Dr. Rush's record shows receipt from an uncle of almost a thousand dollars from 1802 through July 1808. Thomas Baynard died in July 1805. Other payments were surely sent through estate agents such as Rhodes and Otis of Charleston. Dr. Rush, exemplifying the common belief that physicians' handwriting is indecipherable, jots in Baynard's account $1.25 for a pair of shoes. In 1807, he transfers from another book $1,045.33 in cash.

Recording that two tracts of land on the little Juniata (Pennsylvania) were "taken in payment of a debt from Jno. Hall," Rush wrote that he was advised they were of little or no value and had probably been sold for taxes long before. With all his talents and knowledge, Dr. Rush was an inadequate bookkeeper and it is not possible to understand how the estate of Dr. John Hall was administered for the care and education of his son. But Providence was at work to determine that this rootless boy was going to be a scholar and perhaps divine intervention was due to the prayers of his mother.

By the enigmatic statement that he never had a legal guardian, Baynard may have expressed a desire to disregard his ties with the Rushes. It seems odd he barely mentions the illustrious Benjamin Rush who was certainly a legend in his own time. (Those later associates in Monroe County, Indiana who assess Hall as pompous and arrogant may never have known that he had been the charge and cousin of a Founding Father.) No doubt the curious situation in which Hall never possessed what appeared to be a vast fortune is the reason for this disconnect and also the harsh words he hurls toward unnamed people of his formative years.

Hall probably never knew of the correspondence between his uncle Thomas and Dr. Rush; he did in his adult years believe that one of his Baynard uncles had planned to adopt him but that this relative had died. He knew that an uncle had left him enough for a "liberal education," but claimed that dishonest agents had sometimes intercepted his small dividends. (When he wrote that he had relatives who did not know of his existence, and they "found it out when I did not need either their recognition or assistance," was he speaking of the Halls? His other Hall connection to Dr. Rush, his grandmother Ruth who was Dr. Rush's aunt, had died before he was born.) In later years, he would admit to some good fortune in that "claims to lands, supposed to be lost and therefore neglected, have been without any labor of mine, acknowledged, and money paid me for the transfer." Whatever bitterness he had in regard to a lost inheritance was not unjustified as history has proved, but somehow there were enough funds to secure an education.

Chapter 2

Is this Miss Betsey's son?

Baynard Hall, the adult, writes:

> ...if the departed know about
> repentant sinners, my own mother and
> those other mothers did rejoice over the
> returning prodigal. You know my history,
> how I was left an orphan in early infancy.
> But God so ordered that although I
> never had any legal guardian, I was most
> carefully instructed by those sainted
> friends who acted as mothers to the
> deserted child, by them I was imbued
> in the precious elementary doctrines
> of the Christian religion...how came I
> to receive that religious instruction?...it
> was in answer to a Mother's prayer! Thou
> hadst a crushed spirit, my mother! Thy
> little ones in all their widely separated
> graves? Thyself brought down from the

high pinnacle of this world's grandeur to the lowly vale—a stranger far away from thy home in the sunny South. They told me, dear faithful Africans, in after years, how thou wouldst gush into tears when looking on thy sole-remaining, feeble little boy—and pray!...I see thee—a misty dream of the dim past—yet real! I see thee—a stately form—a flowing dress in the fashion of by-gone years! Mother! But alas I should not know thee—thy face I never learned. Yet I have read that –*Prayer!* Years ago it was mine—the heedless child lost it—but God lost it not—He heard and answered.

Pre-eminent in attachment was my mother's nurse. At my mother's marriage, being set free, she accompanied her to the north in the capacity of nurse and housekeeper. She was genuine African— her face was gashed and scarred according to some pagan superstition. In my father's family, the faithful nurse remained till all—father, mother, children, eight or nine in number, lay in the church-yard.

While Hall recognized his maternal roots, he may never have known that his mother was first married to Thomas Elliott, a Hilton Head, South Carolina planter who in his 1786 Will left her two guineas, and for an unborn child four shillings and eight

pence, (shillings and pence in the exact amount of
a Spanish dollar) all in lieu of any other inheritance
from his estate, for reasons he wished to keep to
himself. After the death of Elliott, and the marriage
of Dr. John Hall to Elizabeth, Dr. Hall filed for
letters of administration against the estate. No final
probate records for these estate matters have been
found. Elliott left his real and personal property to
his mother, sister, brother, and brother-in-law, Glen
Drayton. John and Elizabeth were married in the
spring of 1788, likely in the city of Savannah. For
Baynard Hall having no near relatives with whom
he had an intimate relationship, and only Daphne
Peterson, his loyal nanny who may have told him
only what she thought he should know, this may
have been a secret chapter of his parents' lives.

William Baynard, Elizabeth Hall's father, died
in 1773 and left her five slaves and all their future
children. When her widowed mother died shortly
after, she left Elizabeth two "female slaves" with
all of their future children and all the money left
by Elizabeth's father to her mother. Elizabeth was
to inherit one-half of any remainder and the other
half designated to be divided between her brothers
William and Thomas.

The following account tells of one of Hall's visits
to Edisto Island:

> Many years ago, as I was on the point
> of leaving the Island for the North, and
> while entering a boat, a very aged negress
> who had most carefully dressed herself

for the interview in her gayest apparel and most gorgeous turban came near, and looking affectionately into my face, and making a low and graceful curtsy said, 'Is this Miss Betsey's son?...she had been my mother's playmate! But when my mother long years before had left her native South to suffer, to die in the North, Charlotte had taken the last look at her youthful mistress—called according to the usage, 'Miss Betsey,' even after her marriage; and now she looked upon her son! Was it wonderful tears filled my eyes? Could I have hurt or mistreated *that* woman? I am not ashamed to say tears are at this very moment dropping on my paper! This may provoke a sneer that I can stand; but I could not endure myself if there was no love in my soul for that kind, tender, loving negro-woman, who loved my mother and then loved her son.

In my wild oats era, I determined, partly in a fit of burning indignation at what was conceived ill treatment and partly in a fit of boyish heroism, to abscond from a detested employment and become neither more nor less than a—privateersman!...a resolution was taken to immediately enlist on board Moffatt's vessel. Having no day so

opportune, I waited till the coming of
the Sabbath and then, instead of reading
Shakespeare, I called up all the man—
or demon, and wended my way, sullen
and resolved to the wharf. And there lay
the vessel. I may not say there were in
my heart no misgivings, no relentings. I
may not say there were not thoughts of
dear and kind friends that had taught me
prayers, in my dark and tossing spirit—
yes, there was a fierce conflict within…
but what home had I? There were things
in my early days bitter and which often
drove my wayward and proud spirit to
the verge of madness or worse. The
changes in my treatment and hopes
were too sudden and grievous for a boy
to bear philosophically, and with scarce a
friend or adviser.

As I was about to put my foot on her
deck to inquire for the captain, my eye
caught just above the entrance of the
companion-way, two drawn cutlasses
crossed—a sign that she was a vessel of
war! Had no weapons been there, or had
the weapons been pistols, muskets or
any species of fire-arms, my resolution
would not have been shaken; but at
the sight of these drawn swords, in a
moment all my nervous fear of death
from cutting awoke, and I became in an

instant a coward, and I fled! I am afraid of cold steel...but my nerves will stand... scorn and that of a shipload of skeptics and infidels. Because use is made of my idiosyncrasy or of any other natural instrumentality to preserve me from what is worse in reality than mere temporal death—the death of my morals—the care of Providence is not less wonderful, nor less to be thanked.

You know my passion for the theatre in early life. I had once resolved to become a player. And what prevented such a one as I from turning to that unholy profession? How happened that a young man of infidel sentiments, of licentious thoughts, an habitual Sabbath-breaker who spent that sacred time in reading plays and practicing instruments of music, one who for years did not affect to pray even by rote and dared to scoff at things most holy—how happened it that such a person with strong passion for the theatre and with no mean capacity for that employment, and after resolving to go to the managers and seek admission, that such a one should suddenly stop, and far enough away from what is termed 'awakened or converted,' turn away in horror, as if from a deep and frightful abyss? Down deep in his inmost heart were dormant truths, implanted years before, which all of a sudden waked, and said in a still, small voice, and yet as powerful as God's own thunder—Thou has gone to the verge away from God—another step and return is impossible. In the theatres they act on Saturday night till Sabbath morning and during the Sabbath they rehearse to play again on Monday night. Now if thou dost deliberately take *gold* to do all this, it is *selling thy soul to hell!* Did I scoff at this? And why not? My answer is a mother's prayer had been recorded and a special and direct providence recalled the former religious teaching of my second mothers, and made it suddenly and irresistibly efficacious.

Enter their churches: Behold Ethiopia there!

The most affecting of all incidents pertaining to this period was the joy of my mother's African nurse who was then nearly one hundred years old. As years increased I became sensible that if the whole world deserted me, there was yet one heart that ever yearned over me with a mother's strong love—one heart that could almost have dropped its very blood to defend my life. How often when she was seated at the corner of the street selling to school children little parcels of confectionary, have I on approaching seen that dim eye gleam with a sudden light of love while tears ran down that seared face. And how often in despite of myself have I been snatched to that throbbing heart, amidst the wondering looks of the passers. I became ashamed of this then (my tears are often atoning for it now) and in my far-off wanderings from God, I partially forgot, no no, not *forgot*— partially and purposely avoided her! And yet that was not surprising—she was a devoted Christian then—and I was a reprobate! Yes, my mother's nurse was a Christian. For more than thirty years, she belonged to the Baptist church in ___; and by repeating texts and quotations from the Scriptures as they were heard from the pulpit, a stranger, to hear her use the word of God, would have supposed her able to read.

> Well, the change came...in her dark and humble back room, we both kneeled down together—the aged saint and the repentant prodigal, and our souls were united in prayer to the same reconciled Father. That dear saint clasped me in her aged arms, and with streaming eyes exclaimed, "God knows, dear massa, I loved you for old massa's sake, but now I love you for the Lord Jesus's sake!"

This early induction into the caring master, loyal and loving servant experience was the seedbed for Hall's slavery stance and led to his novel *Frank Freeman's Barber Shop* in which a character named Dinah was the personage based on Daphne

Peterson, the nurse to whom he was entrusted by his father. Since there is no indication that Dr. Rush took the toddler into his household, it's almost certain that the boy spent his pre-school years in the home of Daphne Peterson. Hall wrote:

> Believe me that notwithstanding all we hear about the extreme cruelty of slave-owners to their slaves, and the invincible hatred slaves have for their masters, in many cases which is affirmed is a *slanderous and malicious lie*. The attachment between owners and slaves is sometimes like the tie of a tender relationship. Slaves may be found who would almost die for a kind master or mistress. There are negroes that will love the children and the children's children for several successive generations...

Frank Freeman was published in 1852. Hall no doubt read Stowe's *Uncle Tom's Cabin*, which was published in 1852 but appeared in serial form earlier. Hall's Dinah character in his novel is a beloved figure who recites her history as the daughter of an African warrior king along the Gold Coast who had slaves of his own.

Daphne was baptized in the Schuylkill River by Rev. William Rogers, D.D. of the Philadelphia First Baptist Church on September 6, 1803. She was among a number of free blacks who made their home in the possibly most racially and religion-tolerant community in the country, although it was not a classless society. She owned property and it appears from Dr. Rush's accounts that she may have bought a house from him. A dedicated abolitionist, Dr. Rush assisted in founding the Free African Society in Philadelphia in 1787; he may have helped others become owners as he dealt in buying, selling and renting houses. A single, elderly black woman owning her own property in the early 1800s personified William Penn's vision for Philadelphia in ways he couldn't have foreseen.

Daphne Peterson died July 20, 1823; her death certificate lists her age at 94, although Hall states that she reached one hundred years and it's possible that he is correct. She was buried in the First Baptist Cemetery. She had her Will prepared June 29, 1821 naming Dr. James Rush as executor and trustee for Rosina Rolley and her children and Baynard Hall and his children. A stipulation provided that if both died childless and James Rush refused executorship; then one of the other four surviving sons of Dr. Benjamin was requested to execute the Will and share in the estate. Dr. James Rush complied with her wish and quickly—the Will was proved July 21, the day after her death. James was the Treasurer of the U.S. Mint, and like his father was a physician, writer, an avid student of science, and a man the frail and illiterate old woman must have trusted.

Rosina Rolley's identity is unknown. She may have been a relative or companion of Daphne, and perhaps lived in Daphne's house after her death. Rosina Rolley evidently did not survive; the house on North Fifth remained in Baynard Hall's family until the death of his unmarried sister-in-law, Martha Morris Young, in 1866. It is most fitting that 202 N. Fifth Street, Philadelphia is now a part of Independence Mall.

Hall's wild-oats years were not lengthy ones. In his creative storytelling he probably exaggerated his excesses. Before and during those years of late childhood and the teen's dabbling with thoughts of treading the planks of theaters and ship decks, he put a lot of education under his belt in preparation for a life of teacher, musician, writer, and minister. In his words: "It is a mistake to believe that God can only be served in religious ways."

Chapter 3

The End of Education is the Power or Art of Thinking.

In this 21st century, there is no high school on Edisto Island. The Baynards who helped support the care of their nephew in the north can be thanked for supporting John Hall's wish that his son have an education that Dr. Rush thought proper. Dr. Rush enrolled Baynard in a boarding school operated by Presbyterian Reverend D. William Latta 20 miles west of Philadelphia for his elementary training. In his youth Hall worked for a printer and later related that he was awakened to help in "setting up the declaration of war against Great Britain, to appear as an extra sheet." (When there was a threat of British invasion during the War of 1812 perhaps he was among the men and boys who gathered to fortify Philadelphia.)

He thrilled as he composed in the "iron stick" accounts of battles by land and fights at sea. In his books, Baynard Hall shows references to more than a layman's knowledge of printing. Where he worked is never told, but Philadelphia at one time had 55 printing offices, as well as booksellers, bookbinders, newspapers, and papermakers. Philadelphia was overrun with printers along with people working in trades and crafts of all kinds: brewers, bakers, bankers, butchers, blacksmiths, brickmakers, brasiers, coopers, carters, carpenters, clock and comb-makers, cordwaners, chandlers, and coppersmiths and smiths of silver and gold, pewterers, millwrights and wheelwrights, joiners, dyers, and fullers. Either in Philadelphia or Princeton, Hall spent some time in a home as a tutor.

His boyhood in Philadelphia was in a community of movers and shakers where names associated with medicine, law, religion, politics and the arts were internationally known. An observant and intelligent child could mix with a variety of races, religious denominations, political philosophies, and socio-economic levels.

Philadelphians were theater-goers and readers. Even the Pewter Platter Inn had a library. Philadelphia had the first hospital in the colonies, and of course Baynard spent time at one of the busiest seaports in the world—90 miles from the ocean—and in walking distance from any place in town. And what boy living between two rivers did not swim and row the Schuylkill and Delaware? He read adventures: The tales of James Fenimore Cooper whose sister said he was bred in the woods,

Davy Crockett, Indian conquests, explorations, guns and wild game; those adventures were still possible because there was a "far West" of rolling and forested hills, prairies, rivers and streams to cross.

Dr. Rush recorded a payment of $60.00 for a year's tuition at Princeton and $30.00 to Mr. Campbell, when Baynard was a boy. Other payments were made to a D. Scudder who may have boarded or tutored him in the Princeton community during Hall's youth. In an address before the American Whig and Cliosophic Societies at Princeton in 1852, Hall said, "I am again at home—the home of my childhood—the home of my boyhood—the home of my early manhood...the merry troops of girls and boys—those the unselfish Campbell taught and governed in the little white school house...." The associations made at school were likely a surrogate family. Benjamin Rush died when Hall was 14; James Rush, the doctor's son, took on the guardianship. When patriot Benjamin Rush is described as having an evangelical passion for teaching, it is ironic that by life's odd circumstances he never knew his charge who also invested his heart and mind in education, writing, and observing the nature of human beings.

On May 12, 1818, Baynard entered the College of New Jersey (later Princeton University) as a sophomore and was dismissed by his own request exactly a year later. He then entered Union College in Schenectady, New York and graduated in July 1820 with a bachelor's degree and distinguished honors. At Union College he was permanently indoctrinated into the philosophy of its president, Presbyterian minister Eliphalet Nott, who approached students with fatherly affection and disavowed harsh discipline. At Union, William Seward, Lincoln's future Secretary of State, was a classmate. Immediately after graduation from Union, Hall enrolled in Princeton Theological Seminary, having chosen the ministry as his profession. Graduating in September 1823, he was licensed by the Presbyterian Church at Frankford, Pennsylvania in October. But other life-changing events had occurred before these.

Presbyterians would always color Baynard Hall's life and as the settling of America moved westward, so would go the Presbyterians, leaving colleges in their wake.

Chapter 4

*I loved as they say one
can love but once.*

It was a love match. She was one of the daughters of a Philadelphia shipjoiner who would leave his cultured wife a widow with four children. Baynard fell in love with "an amiable and interesting creature." Mary Ann Young was two years and one day older than Baynard Rush Hall when Rev. Samuel Kelsey Nelson, a Presbyterian minister in Danville, Kentucky, officiated at the wedding in May 1820. The couple had been engaged since the groom was 16 years old. He described a romance poignant in its ordinariness:

> ...after the usual courtships, lovers' quarrels, scenes and walks in the garden —(Pratt's), versifications, notes on gilt-edged, flame coloured paper ornamented with cooing doves and little fat dumpling cupids—in short, after the

most approved meltings, misgivings,
misapprehensions...came the customary
Miss-taking—and with consent of friends
east and west we were married.

The couple's walks were on the grounds of
Lemon Hill mansion owned by Henry Pratt. A
setting on the Schuylkill, its former owner was
Robert Morris, known as the financier of the
Revolution (and one of many whose speculation in
land led to bankruptcy). It can be concluded that
the lovers had known each other from childhood
and perhaps in the compactness of Philadelphia,
they had lived in the same neighborhood. In
Philadelphia those who were wealthy went about
their business in close proximity to those who were
not. Mary Ann's widowed mother, Ann Holmes
Young, was an enterprising woman, a teacher, and
was described by two sons-in-law as a beauty, tall,
and obviously having a natural elegance. But never
in all his written works does Baynard Hall go into
detail about his wife. Admitting he "always had a
sense for sweet and beautiful faces," he was also
attracted to intelligence.

Mary Ann was a faithful and long-suffering
companion to the very end. Hers is a story that can
never be faithfully reported, only imagined, and that
would never do justice to what she endured. It is in
Frank Freeman that words describing a love that
is "but once" are found and surely those words are
Hall's tribute to his soulmate, support, and fellow
sufferer in the most unnatural of life's tragedies.

It was a reversal of family fortune that brought Mary Ann's family to Kentucky, following the economic woes in the years after the War of 1812. Meanwhile, she remained in Philadelphia, a student of Daniel Jaudon, another Presbyterian educator who had taught in the College and Academy of Philadelphia, and then established a seminary for young women on Mulberry Street. He was said to have an unrivaled reputation as an instructor and it was noted that obtaining a place in his institution was a privilege. Her education provided Mary Ann with the ability to play Beethoven in the outback of Indiana and conduct classical studies for girls and young women.

Mary Ann and Baynard traveled to Danville after his graduation from Union College, and surrounded by Mary Ann's mother, siblings, and other relatives, they promised to be together for better and what would become the worst of losses.

In that union, Miss Betsey's son, the orphan who had no close blood ties with any other human being, found and was welcomed into a real family.

> "...folk that knew all about three-
> story brick houses in Philadelphia
> ...who had ridden in their own
> carriages and promenaded Chestnut
> Street."

Indiana author Kate Milner Rabb was a columnist for *The Indianapolis Star*. In 1929, she received a letter from a reader, Margaret Carlisle, who found in a box of old books, a copy of *The*

New Purchase which reminded Miss Carlisle that her mother had known the Halls when they lived in Newburgh, New York. (In recollections that are both factual and confused, with events and people churned together, there emerges a hint of another fascinating and lost story.) Miss Carlisle has Mary Ann Hall attending the Girard College of "domestic science," but Stephen Girard's school was for disadvantaged white boys and did not open until 1848, later becoming Girard College in Philadelphia. A vital figure in Baynard Hall's life story is Martha Holmes Doughty, maternal aunt of Mary Ann Young Hall. She occupies a place in the Hall burial plot in Brooklyn, her simple white headstone reading "Aunt Doughty." In Carlisle's passing on of her mother's story, she reports in the Rabb column,

> Aunt Doughty...was an intelligent, bright and wise old lady. Dr. Hall said no household should be without an old lady and a cat. In Aunt Doughty's young girlhood, the family had lived in Philadelphia across the street from our first President. The colored servant would cross the street, rap on the door and inquire if Mrs. X., Aunt Doughty's mother, would be at home to receive Mrs. Washington. Then in the afternoon, Mrs. Washington, attended by the servant carrying her reticule, would cross the street to visit Mrs. X. I never

heard whether they knit or embroidered
or just talked; whether they had tea or
cake and wine; the latter probably.

The Washingtons defied a Pennsylvania law that
prohibited temporary residents holding slaves more
than six months, after which time they had to be
manumitted, by rotating their "colored servants."
That part of the household staff began with eight
and dwindled to one or two during the Washingtons'
time in Philadelphia.

According to the Carlisle story, "one evening
Aunt Doughty sang at a charity concert and sat in
the box with the President and Mrs. Washington,
dressed in white with a white opera cape about
her until she went upon the stage to sing." The
Washingtons frequently attended theater and
Martha Washington was well known for enjoying
the company of young ladies; her husband often
dropped in on her afternoon gatherings at their
home on Market Street, between Fifth and Sixth.

Another anecdotal offering is that Aunt Doughty
took in a runaway slave girl as a house servant. When
scrubbing the front steps the girl was recognized;
whereupon Aunt Doughty sent her out the back
door directing her to the homes of Quakers on the
next street. Later Aunt Doughty is at market; the
girl accompanying a Quaker woman tugs on Aunt
Doughty's dress. Aunt Doughty puts finger to lips
and shakes her head to warn the girl to keep silent.

During Philadelphia's tenure as the capital of
the new nation, George Washington was a respected

but familiar figure about town, and members of Congress gathered in the local taverns.

Martha Doughty was born Martha Holmes who family researchers believe was a daughter of Abel Holmes, Sr. His children included Martha, John, Thomas, and Ann, the siblings who eventually migrated to Indiana, and others. The Abel Holmes family lived in Philadelphia at one time in the vicinity of the Washingtons' residence. As Washington began his second term, Martha Holmes married coppersmith Robert Doughty, Jr. in the Second Presbyterian Church of Philadelphia in May 1793, one of the worst of the plague years in the city; 59 members of the Second Presbyterian died that September. That epidemic took the life of Dolley Payne Todd's husband and a little son; Dolley would become Mrs. James Madison. Perhaps as the young wife of John Todd, she was also acquainted with the Holmes' and others of the "promenaded brick streets and three-story houses," mentioned by Baynard Rush Hall in describing his inlaws. Martha Doughty lost her husband, raised an orphan nephew and, then as many unmarried women did, became companion, nurse, and comfort in family groups where loving hands were needed. Aunt Martha Doughty as "Aunt Kitty" was that feisty, dear, and constant presence in the extended family of Baynard Hall, a symbiotic relationship that lasted until her death at 91 in 1864.

Hall wrote of her,

Aunt Doughty was intended by

nature for a dear delightful old maid;
and she greatly mistook her vocation
by marrying, although nothing but her
being a great favourite with the beaux of
the last century hindered the fulfillment
of her destiny She was the most amiable
and kind-hearted woman....

On March 9, 1797, the Washingtons left for
Mount Vernon and what would not be long years
of retirement from the service of their country. Ann
Holmes Young who had married Nicholas Young
Jr., in the Second Presbyterian Church, was at that
time caring for a toddling daughter Mary Ann, and
awaiting the birth of her only son, John Morris
Young. An enlightened and well-read woman, Ann
probably followed the latest (often two months old)
news of Napoleon from Europe. John M. Young's
birth in September, only four months before his
future brother-in-law Baynard Hall, occurred
during another Yellow Fever outbreak. Dr. Rush
was again wrestling with cause and treatment, and
tirelessly bleeding victims right and left. Enough
lived to convince the doctor that bleeding was good
practice.

Baynard Hall wrote that his wife's people were
"an ancient family and in their day men of substance
and renown." Thomas Holme, a cohort of William
Penn, laid out the early city of Philadelphia. Early
Holmes and Holmes' were working in the precursor
of steel manufacture; others involved in gainful crafts
and trades. They descended from followers of Penn

who looked for religious freedom, good soil, water routes, and relief from war. They may have rubbed elbows in the 1790s with those renowned French *emigres* to Philadelphia following the execution of Louis XVI and Marie Antoinette, including Talleyrand, who promenaded the brick streets and lingered in the bookstalls; Louis Philippe, the Duke of Orleans, and future king of France, and Joseph Bonaparte, the brother of Napoleon.

Sometime after the War of 1812 and during a financial slump which Hall explained as the Holmes family having invested in "certain manufactories" and losing what must have been an irretrievable fortune, it appears that John and Thomas Holmes and other relatives migrated to southern states in search of land in speculative ventures that could quickly turn a profit. Sisters Ann Young and Martha Doughty remained in Philadelphia with their families. After both sisters became widows and were living together, their brother John came to Philadelphia and moved them with Ann's adult, unmarried children to Kentucky.

It is in Kentucky that the saga of *The New Purchase: or, Seven and a Half Years in the Far West* and Baynard Rush Hall's professional life begins. It is the story of Isaac and Elinor Young Reed, lifetime missionaries; John Young, Uncle John and Uncle Thomas Holmes, frontier adventurers; Aunt Martha Doughty and Ann Young, entrepreneurial women; Mary Ann Young, educator and wife of educator and minister Baynard Rush Hall; Martha Young, youngest sister and teacher. It is in that feeder state of Kentucky that many future Hoosiers are gathering; people who do not meet in Indiana for the first time, but who have been friends, neighbors, relatives, and associates before. For many, Indiana will become the feeder state for another westward march.

Baynard Rush Hall left a wealth of information and a dearth of information. What he did leave is enough to form a picture of a remarkable, loving, talented, and high-principled family. They came together and for a short and idyllic time, their lives intertwined in a heavily wooded, spring-fed, back-of-the-beyond wilderness, far from Philadelphia, in a place called Owen County, Indiana near the west fork of a river called White and "shining" because it was so clear.

Chapter 5

Civilized man, and he only,
turns wastes into verdure,
and bids the wilderness blossom.

The Halls were married in the family home in
Danville adjacent to the first building of Centre
College, an institution to which the Presbyterians
pledged a great deal of money. Isaac Reed, a
Presbyterian missionary, was an almost obsessive
traveler, preacher and writer whose evangelical
drive led him to travel 2,480 horseback miles in
1824. He had met Elinor Young at a synod meeting
in Kentucky where perhaps Uncle John Holmes had
been a delegate. The Reeds were also educators.
Elinor Reed, her mother Ann, and younger sister
Martha Morris Young, established a school for young
women in Danville, while Uncle John Holmes was
buying and renting out land, and Isaac was scouting
unchurched territory.

After leaving their Kentucky-based relatives, the Halls returned to Philadelphia; Baynard graduated from Union College in 1820. It was a momentous year. The Indiana Legislature, on paper only, established a state seminary and chose a location in Monroe County in an area Baynard Hall assumed was part of "The New Purchase," a tract of land taking in a huge chunk of the center of the state, but that part of Monroe County fell inside the bottom third and outside The New Purchase. In that year of 1820, Colonel Williamson Dunn, another former Kentucky Presbyterian, became registrar for the Terre Haute land office; Dunn was a brother-in-law of Dr. David Hervey Maxwell, an Indiana legislator and trustee of the proposed seminary.

Elinor and Isaac Reed's first child, Martha Doughty Reed, was born and then leaving wife and baby in Kentucky, Rev. Reed traveled to Indiana where he began the planting of what would be many churches.

Still residing in Philadelphia in the fall of 1820, Mary Ann Hall became pregnant with their first child. He was born in the middle of July during the sizzling summer, escaped the causes of newborn death and was named John. Daphne Peterson made her Will in January 1821, and in that year the American Colonization Society established the African country of Liberia for freed slaves, a move that would have pleased their friend and advocate, Dr. Benjamin Rush, and seemed to many the best solution to a burgeoning problem.

Baynard Hall was completing his three-year Princeton Theological Degree with money a certain adversary will later scoff at Hall's not having earned, but probably some funds were found from his father's estate. What finally occurred in the settlement of his father's affairs and the processing of John Hall's vast land claims is difficult to determine; complete records have not survived.

In the 1820s, Kentucky land deals often required re-surveys and legal action. Uncle John Holmes, experiencing a bank failure and perhaps being unable to collect from some relatives who were renters, sold his land. Isaac Reed, having traveled into Indiana, and his brother-in-law John Young, having been a store merchant in Kentucky and member of surveyor Duff Green's crew even into Missouri, knew there were opportunities north. As early as the spring of 1821, Martha Doughty applied for Owen County land; she bought 80 acres just over the boundary into The New Purchase in February 1822. Isaac Reed and his mother-in-law Ann Young jointly bought an adjacent 80 acres of wild, heavily wooded, sparsely settled Indiana. In November 1822, John Young accompanied his brother-in-law to the federal land office in Terre Haute where Reed and fellow Presbyterian Williamson Dunn, agent, renewed their acquaintance and Isaac signed on for another 80 acres. Land was cheap, a safe investment, and a little money went a long way.

Uncle John Holmes had struck out ahead of the family to establish the settlement in the Owen

County part of The New Purchase and because of a fall from a horse was unable to complete a cabin, but upon his arrival he found his brother Thomas (whom Hall called the "Leatherstocking" of our tribe) with wife Nancy as squatters nearby. This enigmatic turn of events, the discovery of a brother building a shelter on land he did not own, is not explained and perhaps Hall and Reed were just never advised how "Uncle Tommy" came to put up a place in The New Purchase, or didn't consider it important to record; after all, families just know these things.

Before the snows of winter in Philadelphia, 1821, Mary Ann Hall was again pregnant, and the Youngs, Uncle John Holmes, and Aunt Martha Doughty were settled into an "unhewed" log cabin in Owen County. Isaac Reed, on a missionary trip, found the family in the middle of woods with "not a cleared field in sight," and Uncle John recovering from a fever. The staunch Presbyterians had already joined the nuclear congregation of Bethany Church, five or so miles away, where Reed would later preach and Elinor's handwriting can today be discerned in its records. Not looking to be farmers, Uncle John and John Morris Young were planning a store, tanning business and more speculation in land, but none of the Young settlement land was registered in the name of John Holmes.

In the heat of summer, 1822, Baynard and Mary Ann in Philadelphia welcomed a baby girl who survived the weeks and months of vulnerable infancy; while in Jessamine County, Kentucky, Mary Ann's sister Elinor Reed and Isaac buried their five-month-old daughter Ann Young Reed, dead of cholera, in August.

When the Reeds arrived in Owen County from Kentucky in the fall and found an unfinished cabin waiting for them, Isaac later described the scene,

> ...arrived Owen County first of October, covered with timber, entered our home week before Christmas, no loft, no...chinking between the logs above the joice plates...a large wooden chimney place cut out of the end of the house a little above the mantle piece.
>
> The winter of 1822–23 I did not go beyond the bounds of the county except a few times into Monroe and to supply at Bloomington.

In May 1823, the Reed family increased by another daughter, Lydia Ann Lapsley Reed, named for a Presbyterian colleague of her father. The Young settlement, as it came to be known, was growing. Baynard Hall received his degree from Princeton Theological Seminary and was licensed to preach. But before Baynard and Mary Ann Hall joined the family in the far west, the 25-year-old preacher and educator traveled to the south and then experienced a life-changing tragedy.

They...tasted...the wormwood of affliction's cup.

In the fall of 1823, Baynard traveled on business, he wrote, revealing this heartsore time in his life toward the end of his first book, and masking himself as the Reverend Charles Clarence. With his education behind him and his license to preach, he and Mary Ann undoubtedly wished to at least visit her family. But there is a trip to the south. Is it the need to learn more about his father's holdings, or to return to his mother's home to revisit, and is it possible he was also seeking a position as preacher-teacher? He makes no indication he had been offered the Indiana seminary post. The Halls now had two little ones, John, age two, and a daughter whose name has not been found. Leaving his family behind in a boarding house where they had, Hall says, "no immoveables," he was gone four months. In the third person, perhaps making it less painful, he relates the story of his return which was probably in February 1824.

> Mr. Clarence, leaving his wife and two little children went to the south again on business; and after an absence of four months, on returning to his boarding-house in Philadelphia, he was surprised at hearing and seeing no signs of his babes.
>
> His wife, instead of answering in words his eager questions, suddenly threw her arms about his neck, and bursting into an agony of tears, exclaimed—*Both are dead!*—come into

our room, I'll tell you all!

What Mary Ann told her husband, he does not reveal. It is so likely that even she did not have words for the anguish. And at such a moment, how could he remember? The records of Second Presbyterian Church of Philadelphia tell what little can be found. On January 19, 1824, John, age two years and six months, is buried; then on January 29, his sister who is 18 months old slips away; both graves were little mounds in the church's Arch Street Cemetery.

It must be the bulwark of stoicism and faith that enables those who can say in spite of their despair, "The Lord giveth and the Lord taketh away," and that would be the piety of these old-school Presbyterians. They were not alone in bearing the loss of children; the life expectancy for a child under two was never hopeful. When they embarked on their journey to where Mary Ann Young could find the solace of mother, aunt and sisters, and the shared grief of kindred Christian spirit, and Baynard could also lean on the spiritual support of his inlaws, the childless couple were wearing the badges of their bereavement. It was not until 1963 that a vaccination for that malevolent child-killer, measles, was available.

Chapter 6

The time of the journey was late in April.

The deaths of their children surely sealed a decision to relocate; the couple boarded a stagecoach en route to Pittsburgh and in the company of fellow travelers, Hall becomes his own alter ego in his pen name, "Robert Carlton and wife Eliza," and "Charles Clarence," a minister of the gospel going to meet his bride-to-be. With these pseudonyms, Baynard Rush Hall will confuse future readers in mingling facts of his life and experiences between the two fictional characters. Also along on part of the journey is "Colonel Wilmar," who in actuality is General John Moore McCalla, a proponent of black emigration to Liberia. Because he and Hall were acquainted, McCalla may have been another source of material for *Frank Freeman's Barber Shop.*

With vivid descriptions of landscape, passengers, conversations, and valises, baskets, hat boxes, cloaks, sticks, umbrellas "stowed in that humming-bird's nest of a stage," Hall brings that journey across the Schuylkill, the Juniata, Cove Mountain, to McConnel's town in the "crazy, rattling, rickety, old machine" that "rolled and pitched and flapped its curtains, and walloped us." There at the stage house he had the breakfast that is the first of the portrayals of culinary fare that would be quoted years in the future:

> ...the coffee (?) was a libel on diluted soot...the tea (?)...was a perfect imitation of a decoction of clover hay...eggs, too—but it certainly was not without hazard to put them in the mouth before putting them to the nose…but look, here comes a monster of a sausage coiled up like a great greasy eel! Hot rolls...a composition of oak bark on the outside and hot putty within....

Arriving at Pittsburgh, the party then set out on the next leg of their journey by way of choosing a craft: "arks, broadhorns, keelboats, batteaux, canoes and rafts." More a house than a boat, with passengers and a crew of captain and mate (the captain with a five-gallon keg "hugged up under his arm next the heart," and contents undisclosed), the kitchen of the ark outfitted with stores and the cabin,

> …subdivided into parlour and stateroom all is ready!...the sunlight dancing from one sparkling ripple to another, a most delicious April morning...

and in the midst of fragrance and flowers
and sunshine and with those we love for
comrades and those we love awaiting
us, we are entering the glorious land of
sunsets!

...the ark reached the confluence
of the Alleghany and Monongahela
and then one grand circular movement
accomplished, that forced the lordly
cabin to the rear, away, away we floated,
kitchen in the van! Down the current of
the noble, beauteous, glorious Ohio!

Over a week on the river with perfect weather,
Hall wrote,

The ethereal floated on the river's
bosom, while its now unruffled waters
floated our rude vessels. It dwelt in the
dark mirror, where shadow of cliff and
forest pointed to a depth down, down
away, far beyond the sounding line. It
was melting in the blazing river, whence
farewell rays were reflected as the sun
hid behind some tall and precipitous
headland. We heard the unearthly in
the whispers of eddying waters sporting
around us; and in the sweet and thrilling
evening songs of happy birds! We saw
it, till the soul was phrenzied, as gliding
past one island, another in front arose
to intercept, and we were seemingly
shut within a fairy lake, never to find

an egress! And here when the breath of day was done and the songs of the birds hushed...

Hall sat with his flute:

Oh! The pure, sweet, plaintive, joyous, wild, ravishing cries of the echoes...The Muses haunted then the forest-clad banks and cliffs; and startled and pleased with the melody of a strange instrument, they caught its strains—and called to one another, imitating its tones, till they died away in the distance.

At the end of the seventh day, believing themselves to be near Maysville, Kentucky, McCalla and Hall went ahead on a skiff to arrange for land transportation for members of the party; at Maysville both the raft and its party would be "broken up." The two men agreed to take turns rowing and guessed by spelling each other they would soon make port. At the end of nine spells, said Hall, they encountered on a bank, "a full-grown male Buckeye," watching their efforts.

How far to Maysville?"

"About ten miles."

...the recitation in rowing was not ended and we went to spelling it ten times more. We were...perfect by the time we did reach Maysville. I was so pleased with my improvement that from that moment I have never touched an oar.

In a hired driver's two-horse cart, a kind of "mongrel Dearborne" wagon, the Halls were 30 miles north of the Ohio on their way to a "very uncertain part of the New Purchase, about 120 miles in the interior," and beyond the west fork of the White River. Of the early spring with its "buttermilk land, spouty land, mash land, rooty and snaggy land, mud holes—ordinary and extraordinary—quick sands and 'corduroys' woven single and double twill, fords with and without bottom, lo they learn (there are lost rivers that burrow under the ground!')," traveling by land in southern Indiana means "traveling by water, or by both mixed, viz: mud and water."

It is no time at all until Baynard and Mary Ann meet up with honest-to-goodness Hoosiers and in later years when modern writers, critics and professional pursuers of history and social studies decry Hall's observations of local dress, dialect, manners and traditions, then they have not met some of the descendants. The intelligence and innate wisdom of those people cannot be judged by their regional, dialectical speech and idioms. Many who carried for a lifetime their southeastern drawl or peculiar local vocabularies were readers of Shakespeare, Milton, the Bible and other classics and often had the latest books in their homes. Often poor, sometimes illiterate, sometimes crude, yet all mixed together, the salt of the earth.

**"From Loo'ville, I allow?" "No—
from Philadelphia."**

Looking for the next tavern for the night (the driver of the cart not knowing the trails and roads any better than the newcomers he was transporting), the Halls arrive at sunset "with much anxiety at a miserable cabin," and inquire as to the distance to a traveler's rest. The lady of the cabin told them it was a "smart bit yet" and "allowed" as they should stay the night. Hall noted the cabin was not a "facsimile of those in dreams, novels and magazines." It was,

> ...a barbarous rectangle of unhewed and unbarked logs, bound together by gigantic dove-tailing called notching...a roof of thick, ricketty shingles called clapboards which when clapped on were held down by longitudinal poles... interstices of log walls chinked, large chips and small slabs dipping like strata of rocks in geology and then on the chinking was the daubing...

But, "at last we were going really and actually to pass a night in a veritable ritey-ditey cabin—in a vast forest too!"

Assisted by a barefoot, tow-headed little girl whose white hair, Hall wrote, was wisped at the top of the head with a string and horn comb, the cabin's hostess prepared what is familiar to Hoosiers and their forbears of the old southeast, "two fowls, but a moment since kicking and screeching at being killed, doused into the skillet into hot oil where they moved around dismembered, as if indignant now at being fried." The cook "doing up her small

stock of English into Hoosiersms," replied to Mary
Ann Hall's question, "Could girls be hired by the
year?"—"...sorta allow not—most time, you'll have
to work your own ash—hopper." When the husband
of the house and his two sons returned, bacon was
fried and more corn pones, ("hard enough to do
execution from cannon") were served and because
the visitors were "most vulgarly hungry," they ate
supper washed down with "real gineine store tea,
nun of your spice-wood or yarb stuff."

After a night in the cabin in which the males and
females may have been segregated into the several
beds, the seekers of The New Purchase departed
but not before the lady of the cabin opined to
their driver that the "stranger and his woman-body
thinks theirself mighty big-bugs but maybe they
aint got more silver than Squire Snoddy across Big
Bean Creek...." And after witnessing her primitive
culinary talents, Hall quipped, "What French cook
committed suicide because something was not done
'to a turn'?"

Now Baynard Rush Hall and Mary Ann Hall,
late of Philadelphia, have come into the wilderness
where neighborliness and hospitality are almost
a rule, but cultural differences are obvious and
noted, not particularly with rancor, but as a "speak-
your-mind" roughness they will experience over
and again.

The next evening approaching, the party is
refused by a ferry keeper to get them across a stream
because she expects them to find a ford. Unable to

find a low place, they escort themselves on a scow and tie it when they find a place to disembark. Then meeting a group of women and children, they learn they are not far from a preacher's house. Rev. William W. Martin, called a patriarch among Indiana old-school Presbyterians, welcomed a fellow Presbyterian clergyman and company into his home, a home in which travelers were warmly received even though a tavern existed there in the Washington County community of Livonia. Rev. Martin's home with two stories, a shingle roof, corn cribs, smokehouse and barn and "a refreshing fire after the chill damps of the forest" was the residence of six daughters and later three sons. A dilapidated cabin some distance from the buildings bespoke the evolution of the Martins' holdings, but as a pastor "located and permanent of a wooden country," he received almost literally nothing for his ecclesiastical services. The pastor's wife related to Mrs. Hall that she "had not seen ten dollars in notes or silver in seven years."

The lack of recognition of a pastor's needs for himself and his family was a common fault in the backwoods. Baynard proposed a society bearing the title "The-make-congregations-PAY-what-they voluntarily-PROMISE Society." Hall's brother-in-law Isaac Reed would leave Bethany Church in Owen County because he was not paid in cash. Hall writes:

> ...no salary whatsoever, make them
> work, chop wood, plough, ride day

after day and night after night in dim,
perilous endless wilds, bid them preach
in the open air or between two cabins
or in an open barn, or even bar-room,
without notes or preparation...weary,
sick jaded; smoke and suffocate them
on a cold cheerless day with a fire not
within but *without* the house to which
the congregation repair during the
sermon in committees, both for heat and
gossip...

"A workman worthy of his hire" applied more to
common laborers than to preachers and teachers in
the far west. As a matter of fact, there were plenty
of preachers who were attached to no church, and
made their living by other means than spreading
the gospel.

Pastor Martin's girls, Hall noted, were educated
"mainly on Bible principles—living fortunately in
that dark age when everybody's education was not
managed by legislatures and taxes." Perhaps Hall
never knew the outcome of the Martin offspring,
but he would not have been surprised to learn that
of ten, three sons became ministers and five of the
daughters, ministers' wives.

One more day's drive in the creaking cart
northward through more briers, brush, brambles,
over rocks, rills, up and down ravines and hills and
the Halls were closer to their family and the site of
the next seven and a half years of their lives.

Chapter 7

White population very sparse,
mainly very poor...illiterate
prejudiced with all the virtues and vices
belonging to woodsmen.

The Halls did not find themselves among
Yankees when they emerged into the one-mile long,
half-a-mile wide clearing that was the site of the
new town of Bloomington, fictionalized by Baynard
as "Woodville." An "old settlers" reunion report
in 1858 of men who had been in Monroe County,
Indiana by 1838 lists 111 residents of whom only six
were born on the Yankee side of the cultural (not
the literal) Mason-Dixon line.

Coming out of the forests south of the town they
pass the two "unfinished brick buildings, destined
for the use of the future seminary...the smaller house
crammed with somebody's hay and flax...the larger
pouring forth a flock of sheep—a very curious form

for a college to issue its parchments—" Referred to as Big and Little College, Hall describes the smaller building as that intended for the master, and like structures in Pewter Platter Alley back in Philadelphia, "being a sniveling, inconvenient thing, ranged each side a gutter;" and due to the ineptitude of planners and builders, the campus had been denuded of trees. But trees in the far west were more than plentiful and most men were handy with an ax. Hall's aesthetics were steps ahead of his counterparts to whom the destruction of great trees was progress, growth and development. (Hall omits the description of the Little College in the 1855 edition.)

Baynard Hall was mistaken in thinking Bloomington lay in that territory called The New Purchase, but The Purchase was only a short ride away, as perceived at the time. The division and establishment of townships and boundaries continued in Monroe County to as late as 1849.

Into this village which he erroneously described as three years old, "large for its years and dirty as an undisciplined, neglected urchin of the same years, and rough as a motherless cub," Baynard and Mary Ann were "stared at, walked around and remarked upon near at hand by the brave...peeped at by the modest and timid from chinks and openings...why then, we could not conjecture" unless because Hall "wore a hat and was shaved," or because she,

...had on no cap and a cap there
was worn by all wives old and young,

a sign in fact of the conjugal relation, and so it was "suspicioned" if Mrs. Hall was not my wife, she ought to be. The caps most in vogue were made of dark, coarse knotted twine, like cabbage net, and were worn expressly as the wives themselves said—"to save slicking up every day, and to hide dirt."

Already, the Halls are different.

Hall states that "by accident" they meet Dr. David Hervey Maxwell. It will have to remain conjecture whether this was an accidental meeting of the parties, or an intentional meeting of the future first instructor of the seminary and a member of the Board of Trustees who will hire him. Dr. Maxwell, whom Hall described as a true Christian, gentleman, rare jewel, able statesman, skillful and tender physician, once or twice a year would put on his leather breeches, leggin's, moccasins, hunting shirt, fur cap and with long rifle, shot pouch and powder horn, tomahawk and knife, and hie to the uninhabited wilds to hunt. This was a pursuit that Hall came to love and long for when life had transported him far from The Purchase. When the Halls encountered the doctor, he was one of the community's hardy Presbyterians, his three children being the first baptized in the local congregation. Dr. Maxwell had studied medicine in Danville, with Dr. Ephraim McDowell, one of the founders of Centre College and known in medical history as the frontier doctor who, in 1809, performed the first successful removal of an ovarian tumor without anesthetics or antibiotics. (Dr. McDowell's patient, a Kentucky woman, lived long, died in Indiana and is buried in Sullivan County.)

Dr. Maxwell served as a surgeon in the War of 1812 in the company led by his brother-in-law, Williamson Dunn. Among his many accomplishments, Maxwell served as a delegate to the 1816 State Convention from Jefferson County, Indiana. The former slave owner drafted the anti-slavery clause of the Indiana Constitution. The Constitution in his handwriting can be seen every year on Statehood Day at the Indiana State House, trotted out from its home in the Indiana Archives in Indianapolis.

Neither Baynard Hall, Presbyterian minister, nor Dr. David H. Maxwell, Presbyterian physician, would know at that meeting that there would be "town and gown" issues, charges of sectarianism, and a perceived lack of support touching their relationship.

But the Halls could not tarry in Bloomington, and though their driver demanded additional pay over the agreed amount, the day was pleasant and the ridges dry so they continued on their way to the Young settlement. There were maybe less or maybe more than 20 miles to go, as always distance was according to the weather, where the stumps were, and if the travelers could sight the blazes on the trees...trees like great columns "ascending many twenty, many thirty, and some even forty feet with scarce a branch to destroy the symmetry!" The *"circumambitudialitariness"* of them, Hall wrote, "We have sat on stumps measured across nearly ten feet–on counting the concentric circles have found these monsters must have been from seven to eight hundred years old! Trees that have tossed their branches in the sunlight and winds of eight centuries!...Older than Noah."

Come then, I will introduce our settlement.

Gosport, Owen County, Indiana, is a small community on a bluff overlooking White River. It was situated with three favorable elements recommending the site: a navigable river, fertile land, and relative safety from malarial disease. The town did not exist when the Hall relatives arrived in the thickly forested, thinly settled area and began a new stage of their lives on land purchased for homes for themselves and additional land for future profit. The Philadelphians-turned-Kentuckians came to the wilderness where their neighbors, mostly upland Southern stock, were at work clearing fields and establishing homesteads. Their neighbors– "whenever we could find one another," as Hall said—included William Payne and his brother, who deadened trees for a 15-acre clearing and made fence rails in 1823 while their father journeyed to Kentucky to buy farm animals that he drove back to Owen County on hoof.

Thomas Robertson, six feet, three inches and an expert with an ax, hired by another neighbor, split 900 rails in one day for $2.25. The ax in his hand,

Baynard wrote, was like the bow in Paganini's. Tom's land adjoined a parcel belonging to Isaac Reed. Later in 1828, in the newly laid-out town of Gosport, future theologian James Mathes cut and split a thousand rails and was paid $3.00. As the 1820s drew to a close, Gosport was becoming a shipping point with flatboats being poled to New Orleans. (In the spring of 1828, merchant James Gentry down in southern Indiana sent a flatboat loaded with produce to New Orleans manned by his son Allen and Allen's friend, 19-year-old Abe Lincoln. While there, the young men observed a slave auction).

In 1819, Isaac Reed had asked for help from his synod to enable him to perform missionary work among people, "without money...and little stock... living in mud-walled cabins." His vision of serving those who were far from any organized institutions was realized in Indiana and Illinois at an early time, and when the Halls arrived in the Young settlement, Isaac with Elinor at his side was ensconced in a cabin which he named "The Cottage of Peace." Another "patriarchal" cabin housed Elinor's mother Ann Young, Aunt Martha Doughty, and Ann's youngest offspring, Martha Morris Young; John Morris Young, and Uncle John Holmes, as well as a hired girl. Surely this arrangement was planned from the beginning to be the temporary home while the family's financial situation improved. Folks in the far west often started out small.

John Young and John Holmes, having launched

the tannery, had been in business long enough to be entertaining customers from around the area in a time when many settlers did their own processing of leather. Uncle John had come first and owing to a skittish horse had to recover from a broken arm and ribs but thanks to a neighbor's help was back on his feet and started the first cabin into which most of the family had squeezed. In theory, Hall said, it was 20 feet square as measured by ax handle and "seasoned" storekeeper's yardstick; but internally by the Halls' carpets, it was an actual average of 17 feet, one inch in length. Because of Uncle John's injuries and perhaps because winter was approaching, the cabin was completed by hired help, and at a cost of $200.00. Those who knew better said Uncle John had been cheated. From the "laying of the first stick to the topping of the chimney...our cabin could have been finished off for Ten Dollars!"

Baynard and Mary Ann, on the trail to the settlement,

> ...chock full of instructions and with all our windings and turnings...kept our eye steadily on the blazes...three blazes in a perpendicular line on the same tree indicating a legislative road; the single blaze, a settlement or neighborhood road.

> ...I have traveled all day long upon a neighborhood or settlement road and seen neither neighbors nor neighbors' cabins. Such road leads sometimes not

to a settlement in *actu* (under the axe) but to a settlement in *posse i.e.*, (among the possums).

The neophytes in the woods spent four hours going three miles through soggy bottom land learning what the term "slashy" meant. Finally reaching the river bank they were ferried across by a red-haired, barefoot woman who hitched up her petticoats and with legs exposed (looking like dancer Fannie Elssler in bloomers, observed Hall) admirably worked a clumsy scow to their side of the river. Then disembarking with directions from the skipper, off they went further confused by instructions in the vernacular; the full of which, Baynard said, "you could not understand and perhaps might not relish." Before the tannery, across the creek in far west terms became "fornence the tan house over the run."

Moving to the sound of an ax, through a "wonderful wilderness of spicewood, pawpaw, and twenty unknown bushes, briars and weeds," they came to a home where again the kindness of strangers provided lodging for the night. The next morning their host sent them on by way of a shortcut and "the reader will of course conjecture what happened—we lost our way. And by turning aside for logs unstraddleable, brush impenetrable, briars intolerable, and for holes we cared not to fathom," they labored up a steep hill to encounter a meandering rail fence and there met "an almost gigantic yet venerable old gentleman, the very Mr.

Sturgis fornence the tan house over the run, in the very suburbs of the Young settlement" who advises them the trip downhill right into the tan yard would be no more difficult than the drive up.

And so the wagon with driver on foot holding the horse, the horse in a sitting position, the Halls holding each other while sliding and grabbing branches and weeds, they descended into the settlement—Baynard and Mary Ann Hall arriving at their new far western home by "gliding into the open arms" of her astonished brother John and Uncle John of Young and Holmes Tannery. From the "capitol" cabin and the Reed cabin rushed the others.

How we crossed the creek I never knew...But still do I believe we were both *hugged* over!

We met and rejoiced and wept... the daughter is once more upon the bosom of her mother! That morning thanksgiving prayers went up to heaven from three households united...for these families were Christian—and wherever in their many wanderings they halted as pilgrims for a day or a year, there rose the domestic altars. God is everywhere!

Chapter 8

Subdivide 289 square feet of an internal cabin into all the apartments of a commodious mansion.

The Young settlement so known because enterprising John Young was the frontrunner of the family in his desire not only to be a tanner and landowner but also to "sell tape by the yard and buy pork by the cwt." The wiry, five feet-seven, 120-pound "least in his father's house" bachelor had been a storekeeper, a surveyor's assistant, and a woodsman who was ambitious. Digressing in his account of *The New Purchase*, Baynard Hall devoted three chapters to his brother-in-law's adventures. As a youth John was destined for the counting house. He had a business head, bought and sold several lots and parcels of land, and when election time came around, he ran for state legislature successfully to serve in 1828–29 representing Owen and Greene counties. Records of the Indiana House of Representatives show that John Morris Young attended every day of the 13th session beginning December 1, 1828. On January 2, he voted for an act to incorporate Hanover College, an institution of higher learning which grew from a most humble of birthplaces, a log cabin. Sale of Williamson Dunn lots in the town of Hanover helped with funds and Dunn also donated land for the site of the college.

The Young settlement was made up of three cabins and the buildings housing the tanning operation, as well as the separate kitchen cabin for fire protection for the buildings and heat protection for the family in summer, 30 feet from the main house. Reeds' Cottage of Peace was a quarter of a mile north of the tannery. Northeast of the Reed cabin stood the Holmes, Doughty, Young residence, the "patriarchal" cabin, a cabin so rough that the original door hinges (there being only one door for entering and departing) had been made of bacon rinds, replaced after the hounds Brutus and Caesar had rendered them unusable.

Due east about an eighth of a mile was the site on which Uncle Tommy and Aunt Nancy Holmes had squatted! Neighbors counted as those who lived within one mile or ten. Hall called the unsettled land in between, "our commons," the range for hunting, and for the habitats of free-roaming hogs, cows "belled and unbelled," horses yoked and unyoked, the yokes preventing them from jumping *into* enclosures. Fences were to keep animals out as well as in.

"There were deer, wolves, foxes, blue-gray and black—squirrels ditto, ground swine, vulgarly called ground-hogs, and wild turkeys, wild ducks, wild cats, and wild, all the wild what-y'callums: opossums too, up, down, in and under gum trees; snakes, with and without rattles, of all colors...." (An account was given of "three barr" killed, and Hall anecdotes the fright of a woman who encounters a panther and its "pantherines.") John Young voted in the legislature on the issue of keeping or letting go the bounty paid for wolf scalps.

Southeast of the settlement was Bloomington and southwest eight or nine miles was Spencer, "at least in dry times, for the town being on the bottom of White River was, in hard rains, commonly under water, so that a conscientious man dared not then to affirm without a proviso, where Spencer was precisely." It was not until a flood control program in modern times that Spencerians could breathe a sigh of relief that, come spring, there was no worry that the river would flow up Main Street. But in pioneer days the water ways were the highways. John Young served on a legislative committee studying a petition requiring Sullivan County to keep Busseron Creek as a highway.

John shared a space and probably a bed in the partitionless, primitive cabin home with Uncle John Holmes. Ann, her sister Aunt Doughty, and daughter Martha M., shared another small area with Martha sleeping in a trundle bed; that space divided by hanging "pendulous petticoats" also gave the hired girl a place. Hanging a carpet, the Halls created their space. A makeshift library-study-parlor was in front of the fireplace and still in this cramped situation there was room allowed for visitors and strangers—indeed Hall said, "at a pinch, several times" they "packed three bodies of divinity or clerical dignitaries."

The first real window in the cabin went to a "toilette room" that housed combs and hairbrushes and where one could retire to read by the light of the 8 by 10 panes. It was a pantry also and shelved there was a large, antique japanned tray on which were set "anti-tee-total glasses, jelly glasses, the remains of a gilded French china tea set" and other mementos of a former life.

Hall remarked he often found Mary Ann and Aunt Doughty "a handling and a dusting and a refixing the relics...sometimes with tears," remembering dear friends who had come for tea. (Other items belonging to the family had been packed away from the eyes of the curious and for safekeeping.) When Aunt Nancy Holmes brought a heavy cake of sugar-tree sugar and placed it on the overburdened shelf above the nicnacries, the oak pins holding it gave way; shelf and all the heirlooms came crashing down. The only keepsake saved was a small goblet belonging to Hall ancestors and then already over a century old. When Baynard related this homey incident in 1843, he and Mary Ann still possessed the little stemmed wine glass, perhaps the only token left of the worldly goods of Dr. John Hall.

The parlor was fitted with shelves for paint-boxes (because the ladies had taught art) and work bags, baskets, sewing and knitting supplies. Under the floor was the potato hole which could hold 20 bushels. Building some shelves for his own use, Baynard stored his "books in several languages, writings, plates, knives, fiddle, pepper-box, flute, mustard-box, and rosin." In the kitchen cabin were the "vulgar pots, kettles, frying pans, hominy-block; and there cooking, washing, ironing, weaving, pickling, preserving, cake-baking, clear-starching, sugar-refining, candy-making" and the pressing of ruffles were done. As confirmation of these domestic activities, over 160 years later, small bits of metal, a match box, and other detritus of kitchenware surfaced under the plow working the soft earth of Robert Bonness' Owen County farm.

Baynard and Mary Ann Hall moved into the unimproved home to live for a time with five other adults: "all in one cabin?" "Yes," wrote Hall, and he did not mention at that time in 1824, a baby was coming to join its little Reed cousins nearby. He also did not record what was among his writings kept in the back corner "study." Were there journaled notes describing the experiences, adventures, and observations that would become *The New Purchase: or, Seven and a Half Years in the Far West,* or work on a future Latin textbook, or copies of letters back to Philadelphia and Princeton? It was brother-in-law John Young who had written to Baynard proposing the partnership in tanning and storekeeping, and the possibility of something to do with teaching. If Isaac Reed and Uncle John's connections with the Presbyterians who had envisioned an Indiana Seminary were clicking, the entire family may have written encouragement to the Halls in Philadelphia to come at once or sooner. It was advantageous to all of them to assemble the family in one place. However unknowable the future might have been, they shared their kinship, the stability of faith and ownership of land.

(I stood in a small copse of woods and wondered if there were a time warp, could I hear the plaintive notes of a flute at sundown mingling with the night sounds of crickets and cicadas, and other creature noises never heard there since.)

Baynard's first summer in the Purchase was spent learning the "art of preserving hides (grinding bark) and the destruction of hides (rife-shooting)." He wrote detailed description of the bark house wherein the wheel to grind chips was turned by "Old Dick," the Pennsylvania Conestoga wagon horse owned by Uncle John Holmes. Dick had a personality all his own and when Hall slipped away to fire at squirrels, Dick would also take a work break. He ate the pigs' food and pies off the windowsill, carried men and boys double and treble but loved the girls so "females might be packed from stem to stern...no saddle or bridle needed; the passengers on the forecastle holding by the mane, those on the poop, by the helm, and those amidships sittin a' la squaw, with ankles on both sides." Dick could plow, pull a cart, gee and haw the correct way when the driver had jerked instead of tugged, and he provided rides to mill, meetings, Spencer and Bloomington. Those who examined the length of the teeth of the aged "hoss beast" estimated him to be 16 or 26 or 30 or 40 years old, Hall said, but his obvious love of that horse made old Dick ageless.

Young and Hall bought hides at higher prices than were paid at Bloomington and Spencer, thereby guaranteeing some success at the tanning business as well as increasing their social connections.

All...who came to our tannery and store...came...armed, and rarely did a customer go till his rifle had been tried at a mark, living or dead, and we had listened to achievements it had done and could do again. In the corner of my bed chamber a genuine New Purchase rifle! And all the forest equipments: otter skin bullet pouch, scalping knife in a sheath adorned with porcupine quills, a savage little hatchet, a powder horn and its loader of deer-horn, tied on with a deer sinew and holding enough to prime a shotgun, a mold running three hundred and twenty-five to the pound, wipers, an iron hook to tote squirrels....

Hall realized his boyhood dream of life in the

woods with unlimited hunting and the thrill of drawing a bead and hitting the mark. Bagging a squirrel stretched out on a limb, hidden by thick branches and leaves, required a true marksman's eye.

The Sabbath was made for man, and women and children and because Rev. Isaac Reed held meetings "in all directions, over and above the regular monthly ones at the Young settlement" where house church was held, and on three successive Sundays at the Payne (Steele) settlement, everyone came "from all quarters of the woods along roads, traces, paths or shortcuts." Horses came to preaching, and Dick "never did so look like a family horse as on Sundays when he usually carried much of our family on his back." The family attended other meetings as well, including those presided over by Baptists and Methodists. Hall said of some of the meetings, those not presided over by Presbyterians, "Most of what was done was to revile others and glorify ourselves." In 1821, Reed became the Bethany Presbyterian's first pastor, the church instigated by Steeles and other residents not far away, although the little congregation was already a year old.

Folks came to the church meetings with different agendas from announcing the straying off of livestock and rewards for the finding, to the young people for whom it is "the grand sparking time," the young men looking for "a most powerful heap of gals." For the women of the Young settlement, all of whom were competent to teach the Scriptures, the

Sabbath must have been a day of quiet reflection and relief from weekday chores with time for visiting with other women at "meeting." Ann Young, past 60, suffered from a long-term femoral aneurysm and relied on her sister Martha Doughty, and daughters Martha, Elinor and Mary Ann, to manage the household work, cooking, preserving, laundry, soap-making and all the drudgery life demanded of women. Elinor had two little ones and Mary Ann was in her third pregnancy.

In the few years that Ann and Martha had lived the primitive life, they had learned some of the ways of the woods. Martha (Aunt Doughty), making sausages, reprimanded the hired girl for throwing out the "guts" to be used for casings, sometimes did the milking, and in being able to interpret what doctors said was encouraged by a neighbor to become a physician herself!

Elinor Reed, whom Baynard fondly called Ellen, was again alone with her children while Isaac resumed his riding the wilderness preaching, baptizing, and no doubt marrying and burying, in all manner of weather and often coming home depleted and ill, but keeping the vow he made at his ordination: "I am thine, Lord, forever."

What these women endured could only be written by them, but they did not leave us their memories. "Amid rough huts, rude furniture, coarse food, and homespun clothes," Hall wrote, "the man who has *practiced* doing with little, and is fully satisfied with it...is superior to the man...of large fortune and of many wants." To Hall, "a sojourn in the woods made better the man who returned to the East and if the East had forgotten him, why the time in the Purchase strengthened him to not give a fig!" It is to the credit of the men of the Young settlement that the women did not have to tend the children, fill the ash-hopper, make the clothes, boil the clothes, slop the pigs, help with butchering, hoe the garden, sweep the floors, and kill the snakes alone; they were willing to employ the neighbor girls. Many of these chores consumed the whole blessed, live-long day, and had to be done over the next.

There were unforgettable people in the Purchase, among them the Brasiers or the Ashers, whom Hall tags as Ashfords, "remarkable for nice housekeeping and for cleanliness of person." Frugal Owen Countians, they had turned nettleweed into a substitute flax and wove it into cloth. They had a daughter Susan, a confidante of Martha Morris Young, and a prospective bride. When the day of the wedding came, the settlement made the two-miles-plus trip to the bride's home by horseback. Uncles John and Tommy leading the way, clearing brush, letting down fences; Ann and Aunt Doughty "riding twice" on Kate, the grey mare, "queen of horses." Elinor Young on a neighbor's horse held Lydia in front with little Martha behind; Mary Ann, Martha M. and Aunt Nancy on Freckled Ginney, and Old Dick with three hired gals also "riding thrice." John

Young and Baynard brought up the rear, putting the fences back, and making sure Dick didn't dawdle or wander off to look for pies.

A very little stranger
(and a small doctor).

In a letter to publisher J.R. Nunemacher in regard to the reprinting of *The New Purchase* in 1855, Baynard promises a key to the real identity of people and places, but true to his enigmatic practice, he does not tell all. "Old Dick is Old Dick," he wrote, and reveals that Dr. Pillbox is Dr. Jocelyn of Owen County. He is partially right except that Pillbox is Dr. Amasa Joslin. Hall portrays an unforgettable character in this "dwarf Esculapius," who was, "exactly one yard, one foot and ten inches—low." No corroboration of the doctor's short stature exists, but documentation of his many civic activities as an early settler and probably as Owen's first physician can be found. His practice extended into two adjoining counties. It was Dr. Joslin's "additmentalities and elongated elaborifications of coxicalities" (1855 ed.) that caused the frequently ailing neighbor woman to send for Aunt Doughty to be the "little doctur's intarpreetur." Precipitating the house call by Dr. Joslin was the pending arrival of a daughter "who bounced in among us...by surprise...and about two o'clock one morning," Hall quipped, "a curious figure somewhere had been missed and the young lady gave an unexpected notice in some mysterious way of her intention to join our colony, precisely one week too soon." It may be that somehow Mary Ann Hall had (in the parlance of old wives) lost her notched stick. But as if almost to deny the existence of the two children dead of disease in Philadelphia early in 1824, Hall wrote of the unexpected birth day, "a common case I am informed with all that have the right of primogeniture; others are better arithmeticians."

It had been arranged that Dr. Maxwell would come from Bloomington for the birth, but at nine o'clock at night John Young, about to be an uncle again, was on board Old Dick "scampering away at...six miles per hour to Spencer, half as far as Bloomington," returning with Dr. Joslin at three o'clock in the morning. The doctor traveled on a horse large in size further dwarfing its rider who sat in saddle between two "hugeous leather cartouch-boxes made for bottles, barks, lint, forceps...and above all for the pills and powders," and possibly ingredients for poultices that the doctor termed "cataplasms." Dr. Joslin's business increased during those seasonal returns of "fever 'n ager," when people came to him for "dosts of calomy and jolop." Disdainful of Thompsonian medicine and "steam" doctors, the Halls had to settle for this physician who had "never-failing remedies for fevers of every type, grade and color; intermittent, remittent, nonitent, bilious, antibilious, red, saffron, and yellow!" Dr. Joslin was called or visited when home treatments of herbs, barks and berries failed. With tongue in cheek, Baynard took note that the good

doctor was licensed by the state, and did not allow
his Spencer landlord, James Montgomery Higgins
Allison (also the postmaster), to keep ducks; no
medical practitioner wants to hear anything about
quacks.

Reading "external symptoms" upon arriving at
the patriarchal cabin wherein the newest member
of the family was by then snuggled with her mother,
the doctor,

> on hearing an infantile cry which
> had commenced just an hour before his
> arrival, and broken out at intervals since,
> he concluded, and without feeling any
> body's pulse or inspecting any body's
> tongue, or asking a question, but with
> a very grand and imposing air, said 'the
> lady was as well as could be expected.'

After pronouncing nature had done its work,
Dr. Joslin ordered,

> ...a few grains of his soporific sleep-
> producing powder to induce a state of
> somnorific quiescence, because he was
> decidedly of opinion that with proper
> care and no misfortunate reactions, the
> lady would without dubiety become
> convalescent in the ordinary time. And
> would you believe it, dear reader?—all
> came to pass precisely as he predicted—
> and stranger yet...without the aid of the
> soporific powder.

Hall, no doubt chuckling as he wrote it, said he

never mixed the powder and then "to atone and for fear some living creature might accidentally swallow it all at once," he put the whole paper of somnorific quiescence into the fire. Baynard and Mary Ann gave the name Elizabeth to the newborn in honor of her paternal grandmother.

While Mary Ann kept to her childbed convalescence for two weeks, Aunt Doughty and Martha M. may have cared for her and the baby. Ann Young embraced another granddaughter, there not being a son born into the extended family for some time ahead, and one she would not see. Uncle John Holmes, childless and gaining in years, no doubt served as surrogate grandfather to the little girls in the Young settlement. Elinor Reed was happy to have a niece and a playmate for her daughters. Uncle Isaac Reed, not at home to record the birth in his journal, could not foresee the painful, troubled time at the college when he would preach "...at the burial of Miss Elizabeth Hall, only daughter of the Rev. B.R. Hall and Mrs. M.A. Hall. She died of scarlet fever at Bloomington, Indiana, June 2, 1832, being eight years old."

Chapter 9

*The reader will readily perceive
a good deal of commonplace...*

Uncle John Holmes was one of the lay delegates in meetings of the Presbytery, lay delegates whom Hall pointed out did not have equal footing with the clergy in the hierarchy of Presbyterian government, but were assigned to bring in pitchers of water, keep a fire on the hearth and contribute each 25 cents *cash* to the sub-treasury.

Uncle Tommy Holmes, a kind of jack-leg preacher himself, according to Hall, could do Welsh evangelist Christmas Evans' almanac sermon nearly as well as Christmas himself, and thence among the "Baptistis," as Uncle Tommy called them, the old gentleman was venerated. Among the learned clergy of the settlement, however, it was preferred that Uncle Tommy recite the sermons of others and not his own even though he was endowed with "pathos and unction." The Ashford wedding dinner, attended by about 60 guests, was delayed while Uncle Tommy related a yarn that *illusterated* (Uncle Tommy's word) "the fillosofee that makes a man keep going round and round when he's lost," a yarn that takes six pages to tell.

Cold weather moved into Indiana and evenings were spent cracking nuts and jokes, Baynard related, and visiting Uncle Tommy and Aunt Nancy's "darling little" 14 feet by 10 cabin on the creek, conversing with Isaac Reed on matters both clerical and secular, making plans, hearing adventures or reading aloud. Doubtless the family was also entertained by flute and violin renditions performed by Hall and singing led by Aunt Doughty. In Uncle Tommy's cabin where books had been read "kiver to kiver" and some so used that they were read "clean through the kivers," after a hunt, "the neatness, quiet, cleanliness and comfort, the wild independence of this nest of a cabin...the stories, all, all were so like the dreams of my boyhood! How happy Uncle Tommy, now more than seventy and Aunt Nancy, more than sixty... happy in themselves, in one another, in their home, and their scriptural hopes of the future life." And supper: "coffee, cornbread, butter, eggs, short-cakes and venison steaks!...away with your Astor House and Merchant's Hotel, and Dandies' Taverns; if you *do* want to know how venison steaks *do* taste—go to Aunt Nancy!"

In Uncle John's "patriarchal cabin" there was no center table, so the "grand family lamp was suspended in the center of the parlor and around this we either sat as an Iceland family, or raising the carpet barriers, we lolled on the nearest beds, in couch and sofa and ottoman style." During the short and gloomy days of Indiana winter, Hall made the closets for Isaac Reed's study and his own, two shuttles for the loom, one too light, however, the other, too heavy; and aided in putting in and taking out a piece thus becoming adept in the mysteries of woof and warp, hanks, reels and cuts. He mended water sleds, hunted turkeys, missed killing two deer for want of a rifle, played the flute, practiced the fiddle and every so many other things and what-nots. He took lessons in axecraft until he had "larned the sling o' the axe," and could execute a cord a day and "in a moment lay two logs out of one."

Wood being plentiful everywhere and to show the grand scale on which "we do even small matters out here," building a fire first required a cabin built for a fire with a fireplace constituting nearly one whole end of the cabin, then "we must have wood, not by the cord, but by the acre." John Young and Hall were the procurers of the back-log of beech, the greener the better, about seven feet long and two in diameter, rolled to the door with handspikes and with the help of Uncle John rolled, lifted, pushed and coaxed into the center of the parlor while the men rested and caught their breath. Next came the second-story back log and the forestick. Chips of various sizes, a bushel of burning coals, bits of small trees...the whole being capped and climactirized with a brush heap. The romance of a huge fireplace, a roaring fire, all in nostalgic reverie by Hall who, in his home in the east writing *The New Purchase,* complains:

> ...our young woman now, in here, keeps everything in the shape of poker, and scraper, and tong, single or double out of my way, and when the grate or stove needs a little tussling, in comes *she* with some iron article or other; but always on going out takes the article with her—for "fear Mr. Hall will spile her fire". Don't lecture me about furnaces and flues and patent grates and ranges... give me my all-burn and no-save fire of beech and sugar and chip and brush— hand back my tong—let me poke once more! Oh! Let me hear and see once more before I die a glorious flame roaring up a stick-chimney...on this cold Thursday, thermometer two and a half inches below zero, let me stand by my cabin fire and be heated once more through and through. Oh, the luxury of lying in bed and looking from behind our Scotch wall on that fire.

But in the settlement waiting for spring, Hall's "grand employment" was reviewing all his college studies, and then he makes the oft-quoted and denied statement, "I was the very first man since the creation of the world that read Greek in The

New Purchase." At the time when he was poring over Virgil and Homer, he may have been the only one in his particular part of The Purchase. This claim may have been another point in Hall's self-defense and justified.

> It was I that first made the apostles
> talk out there in their own language! That
> made the primal woods resonant with
> *Tyture tu patulae recubans sub tegmine
> fagi!* or thunder with Demosthenes!
> That first addressed the revereful trees
> in the majestic words of Plato...that first
> taught those listening trees the names
> of the Hebrew and Chaldaic alphabets,
> or made them roar like the sea with the
> *popupholosboio thalasses*!

It was in November that the trustees of the seminary (first provided for by legislation in 1820) made a decision. The time was right to staff the new institution. When trustee Dr. Maxwell, instrumental in the hiring of Baynard Rush Hall as the first principal and only faculty of the new Indiana Seminary at Bloomington, was charged with sectarianism in the employment of a fellow Presbyterian and a minister at that, the discontents overlooked the fact that Hall was the most promising candidate. He an educated classical scholar, a gregarious and intelligent young man with an unusually observant eye, eloquent and sensitive; a man with humor, pathos and passion for learning and teaching— right there and willing to settle into a permanent position at evidently

whatever pay the State was willing to offer. And
Baynard Rush Hall put it in writing that he would
have stayed to the end of his life.

Chapter 10

*Men of science may, indeed,
fall into errors.*

In the October 1823 term of the Owen County Court, an indictment against Paris Dunning and Enos Lowe was brought by the State of Indiana on the charge of digging up a human body. Dunning, 17, and Lowe, 19, were Monroe County boys and said to be students of Dr. John M. Jenkins of Bloomington who was a seminary trustee. But in the story related by Hall, a doctor's nephew was also a culprit. Hall has the "nevy" as James Anderson Maxwell, nephew of Dr. David Maxwell, and another budding doctor. The body was that of an Indian, Big Fire, always referred to as a chief in local lore, who died while a band was camped not far from the Young settlement. (He has been described as a Delaware, a Miami, or a Shawnee.) This event likely played out in the summer of 1823 while tribes were still being dispersed to the west and moved out of their homes by way of clever treaties. Hall expressed his sympathies for the displaced people. Of the gravesite he wrote, "That spot I could never pass without feeling myself on hallowed ground, often contemplating the scene with indescribable emotion—ay, more than once with unbidden tears."

Titled "Hunting Shirt Andy's Story," Hall in exaggerated dialect related the tale of the young men who came to exhume the chief for an anatomical specimen. The identity of "Andy," who Hall said repeated this story in Uncle John's cabin, has been impossible to determine but some of the actual identities of participants in the story were revealed in an article published in a Gosport newspaper, which was then reprinted in a Spencer paper in 1874.

Andy told Hall,

…case you put it in your book, don't let on about thare nameses—as the doctor's nevy is a most powerful clever feller and tended me arter the agy and charged me most nuthin at all although he kim more nor once all the way more nor twenty miles….

"Well, we heern the two was a comin to git up Blue Fire, and bile him for a natumy…and all us neighbours was powerful mad about it, as cos couldn't they allow the poor Injin to lay in his

grave; and as cos the Injins still a sort
a squattin and campin round, mought
hear on it, and it moughtn't be so good
for folks's consarns then.

Andy, replete in his trademark costume, spun
how he and "Bill Roland" decided to paint and
dress like Indians and with weapons lie low near
the grave awaiting the resurrectionists.

We lays teetotally still and they
goes fust and fassens their hossis to the
swinging branch of that thare sugar west
o the place, and then goes and begins a
takin down the pen, and then they gits it
down, they off's coats and begins a diggin
like the very divil. And jist then we raises
up a sort a on our kneeses and all draws
bead at that knot in that thare beech at
the tail ind of the grave....

...then we lets three balls crack-wack
right into the knot...and then out jumps
we and raises the yell, with tomhoks
agoin to fling—. I've seed runnin in my
days...but if them chaps didn't git along
as if old Sattin was ahind 'em.... Well,
they divides and the doctor's nevy, he
tuk strate up stream...but tother chap
kep right study ahead slash through
weeds and briars to the river and me
slam smack arter him as cos I was afeerd
he'd run in and git drownded for thar's
where the water is deepish, and jist

about where you'd swim'd your hoss.... If he didn't make the brush crack and streak off like a herd of buffalo...and in he splash'd kerslush...and waded and swim'd and splashed and scrabbled even ahead rite strate across and up to tother bank.... As you may naterally allow, the hull settlement over thare was a sort a sker'd and sent out scouts and hunters... but when it was found how it all was exactly, then if they warn't a mighty powerful heap of laffin...

Andy explained that afterward the doctor's nephew,

...was good pluck for he gits another chap to help and two days arter when we warn't a watchin, he digs out the poor Ingin and totes him over to Bloomington and biled him up for a natumy for their shop arter all...

When Hall's narrative of Andy's story is reprinted, the Gosport editor writes, "We ought in charity probably conclude that they did this more on account of their enthusiasm in the cause of science and a desire to learn, to benefit the living, rather than from a want of regard for the rights of the dead."

Was it Dunning and Lowe who had had spent the night at Ephraim Goss' home and next morning were directed to the grave by Goss? Three men, Ben Arnold, Ben Fuller and John Roland, learned the plan and decided to scare the daylights out of the apprentice doctors and successfully did so. Facts were, the newspaper stated, Dunning never did know how he got across the river, nor did he learn how the proposed theft was discovered until as Paris C. Dunning, attorney at law, he was examining Joseph E. Goss during a court case. Joseph, who was a child at the time of the grave robbery, was on the stand and questioned by Dunning for a while. (This trial was surely the 1867 Johns murder trial.) But lawyer Dunning's mind seemed to be wandering from the case at hand. Finally, turning abruptly to the judge, he asked permission to ask the witness a question not connected with the trial.

"Joseph, was not you in the corn crib that morning when I asked your father where Big Fire's grave was?"

Another court entry in the October 1823 term stated if the defendants Dunning and Lowe "be taken, they may be discharged on recognizance for their appearances on the first day of the next term to answer the indictment," for the sum of fifty dollars each. The next entry in the docket is in the November 1824 term of the Owen court, the trial of the State of Indiana versus teenage Paris Dunning on the indictment of exhuming a human body. It did not include the name of Enos Lowe, nor was James A. Maxwell mentioned. A jury of "twelve good and lawful men," residents of the Gosport neighborhood, found the defendant, future Governor Dunning, not guilty. Paris Dunning gave up medicine for law, earning a reputation as a competent criminal lawyer. He served in the Indiana legislature, on the Board of Indiana University Trustees, as lieutenant governor and governor of Indiana. The doctor's nephew, Baynard Hall reported years later, was James A. Maxwell, charter seminary student and son of James Anderson Maxwell, Sr. While James A. was a nephew of Dr. David Maxwell, it seems in the transmitting of this narrative, Hall perhaps placed him in the story when he did not actually belong, or possibly James was the second recruit returning the next day.

Enos Lowe had a long and distinguished career as a family physician and Civil War surgeon serving with his son General William Lowe, and earning high praise for his dedication to his patients and his practice. He and brother Jesse were founders of the city of Omaha, Nebraska, and both are prominent and respected figures in Nebraska history. (With their brother Jacob, they were sons of William Lowe who was opposed to the Presbyterian faculty and to Dr. Maxwell's political philosophy. Jacob Lowe was "Brig. Gen. Jacobus" in *The New Purchase*.)

At an unknown date, Dr. Lowe donated Big Fire's skull which ended up in the Academy of Natural Sciences of Philadelphia. Background information reported in 1855 claimed that the skull had been sent to Dr. Ashbel Clapp of New Albany, Indiana. He then passed it to Dr. Samuel Morgan, noted Philadelphia physician-ethnologist, who studied the skulls of over 400 Native Americans and wrote *Crania America*. The remains of Big Fire eventually came to the University of Pennsylvania Museum of Archaeology and Anthropology; in 2003, the Miami Tribe of Oklahoma with support of the Peoria Tribe of Oklahoma requested and was granted repatriation of the skull.

Dr. James Anderson Maxwell Jr., one of the several physicians in the Maxwell family, lived in Grand Gulf, Mississippi, and died a young man.

Hunting Shirt Andy's ornamented apparel, decorated with dyed porcupine quills, birds' and beasts' claws, distinguished him from his second cousin, "White-Andy," Hall said, "so named because he lived like the rest of us civilized woodsmen in a cabin."

In 1839, Sauk chief Black Hawk's grave was robbed and bones, cleaned and varnished, were later given to the Sauks who asked the governor of Nebraska to keep them. The governor placed the skeleton of Black Hawk into the care of Dr. Enos Lowe.

Chapter 11

We were now fully under weigh at Bloomington.

The date the Halls moved to Bloomington, leaving the little "self-exiled company of the settlement" is unclear. Shuffling events and vague in locations, Baynard's stories leave the impression he lived in the Young settlement longer than they were actually there. He mentions moving into Dr. Maxwell's house, perhaps a rental before the seminary residence was completely habitable. The residents of the patriarchal cabin stayed behind, but Martha M. Young accompanied the Halls to Monroe County where she and sister Mary Ann planned to establish a school for young ladies; Aunt Doughty came along to get everyone "fixed" into the new home. John Young remained in Owen County where he was often called for jury duty, continued the tannery and bought produce for the New

Orleans market. At this time, Hall reported, John was a candidate for county clerk. On the occasion of the move, Aunt Doughty went in the wagon with the Halls and baby girl, Old Dick pulling the loaded wagon for the venerable horse's last venture with the man who so loved him. Dick returned to the tannery but would not grind the bark without company, John Young being too busy with other pursuits, and so was sold and "ended his earthly career as he had begun, as a wagoner's wheel-horse."

> I, standing at our upper story back
> window, cried out, as he wheeled into
> his retrograde position—Good-bye,
> Dick, good bye!

Hall describes fastening up copies of their prospectus for the girls' school at the post office, courthouse, jail, doctor's office and other public sites, handbills which he with his printer's experience designed himself; then he set out for Louisville to lay in goods and also to obtain a piano for their school. Hall indicates they kept a store; it can only be surmised that a room in their residence served as such, and it may be that it was the Bloomington annex of the John Young mercantile business.

The "pianaforty"or pi-anna was a sensation in Bloomington, and on that instrument Mary Ann Young played Beethoven for guests and the uninvited who popped in and out unceremoniously to ask her to play "to the amazement and delight of our native visitors, who, considering the notes of the piano as those of invitation came by day or night, not only around the window, but into the entry, and even into the parlour itself." A violinist, Hall welcomed into his home lawyer James Whitcomb, a future governor. With disdain for what he deemed selfishness and moral cowardice, Baynard makes him "Insidias Cutswell." Whitcomb brings his violin; he is "no mean performer on the instrument," said Hall. Insidias is redeemed later in life: "He became a religious man before he died," Hall wrote. Back at the settlement, the matriarch of the family, Ann Young, failing in health, again welcomed a granddaughter, Sarah Reed, born June l; another girl filled the vacuum left by baby Elizabeth's transfer to the college town. Rev. Hall baptized that niece at Bethany Church on July 23, 1825.

On August 3, the annual synod meeting was held at Vincennes. Rev. Hall was employed as a missionary for six weeks and was paid for three during which he rode 250 miles and preached 12 sermons, according to Isaac Reed. It may have been during that missionary tour that Hall preached at a saw mill describing the incident as an extemporaneous sermon by "Mr. Merry." When using even the most simple terms, he perceived that his audience of the saw-miller, Mr. Forster, two workmen, and three hunters who dropped in ("in all six sinners") were less than interested. He stopped preaching and started talking, comparing spiritual conditions to marksmanship and shooting matches—a departure from the stilted style of prepared sermons—and winning the favor of individuals characterized as not "powerful gospel greedy."

A visit in the home of William Conner, interpreter and Indian agent, may have occurred during this tour, although Hall's description of this incident does not fit with facts. He used the name Mr. Redwhite, but in the key said he was John Conner. John was William's brother, and Hall errs in the description of Conner's wife, linking her to the Wyoming massacre of 1778 in Pennsylvania. Neither John nor William had a wife who was a victim of that attack, but the historic event could have been a topic of conversation. Whether the story was embellished, or whether Hall confused the two brothers, it is very possible he was a guest in William's home. Hall's description is a reflection of the William Conner house. (John Conner died April 1826; Rev. George Bush officiated at the funeral.)

Preaching for the local congregation, Hall conducted two services on Sundays and sometimes others through the week, visited the sick and the dying, and attended funerals. Never refusing what he felt was his duty to others, he sat in his congregation and preached when too ill to stand, introduced a course of Greek that kept his lamp burning until two o'clock for many months, gave all the knowledge of music he possessed to his students, and "gratuitously, and at extra hours to certain teachers of ordinary schools, and some of these former opponents." Glaringly self-serving is that litany of efforts, yet the preacher-teacher was reputed to be generous and conscientious in all his dealings throughout his career. His only inquiry, he said, was how could he make this institution better, wherever he served.

Mrs. Hall, the mother of a one-year-old and soon to fill that unpaid position, the pastor's wife, "began more clearly to understand an elegant phrase, addressed to her at our entrance into the wooden country—'the working of one's own ash-hopper.'" Mary Ann was finding problems with hired girls whose work often had to be done over, ("clothes abandoned in the first suds") and who ran off to the latest religious revival meetings. Aunt Doughty had stayed awhile to help get the household in order, but returned to the settlement in the fall, at which time the Halls paid a "flying visit."

John Young had been defeated in the clerk's race by a majority of eleven votes, but Baynard wrote that his brother-in-law now had time to collect debts due,

> Young & Co., a business that would have been easy and pleasant but for two small obstacles; most of our debtors who were very willing indeed to pay, had no visible property; and the rest were even invisible themselves! For, pleased with the credit system in the Purchase, they had gone to try it elsewhere, and had become suddenly so unmindful of "the powerfullest smartest man and darndest cleverest feller in the county,"

as to go away without one tender adieu!
The fact is, our *dear* old friends had
absquatulated.

Hall was correct in that those willing to pay had
no visible property. Cash in hand was a rarity and
likely the business of Young & Co., storekeepers
and tanners, had all the products on hand that were
needed to keep their endeavors going. John M.
Young at some time moved his store into the growing
village of Gosport on the bluff, and continued buying
and selling land. It was apparent that Isaac Reed
was becoming exhausted, and receiving practically
nothing from his pastoring of Bethany Presbyterian
in Montgomery Township, Owen County, he was
considering a return to the east, leaving behind his
wilderness travels and fledgling churches. In July
1825, he wrote in resignation figuratively that he
was leaving because of the "entire inadequacy of
support from my congregation; I have not had a
dollar in money in nearly two years," but he waited six
months to make it official. Uncle Tommy and Aunt
Nancy Holmes had an eye toward building their next
cabin on Lake Michigan. "Squaterees" such as they
often left no written records or other paper
trail behind to mark their next trek into another
wilderness.

In the Reed cabin the Reverends Reed, Hall,
and George Bush met in 1825 to form the Wabash
Presbytery branched off the Salem Presbytery,
which had held its first meeting in Washington
County, Indiana in April 1824. Isaac Reed and

John Holmes had attended that meeting in the community of Salem. Had Baynard Hall been in Owen County early that April, surely he would have been present with the august body of prominent Presbyterian clergy and the active elders who gathered at Salem.

In April 1825, Reed traveled from a Daviess County meeting to Bloomington to ordain the Reverend Baynard R. Hall as pastor of the local congregation, an event important enough to warrant an announcement in the *Gazette*. Reed says the ceremony on the 13th took place in the seminary building.

For filling the Bloomington pulpit, Hall was hired at a salary of $150.00 per year to be paid in goods, an income of gifts and offerings of such possibilities as beeswax, fruits, nuts and berries in season, jams and jellies, eggs, herbs and goose feathers, the products of butchering and the occasional fat hen or skinny rooster centerpiece for Sunday dinners? In his estimation, that income amounted to about $50.00. He did not keep his position as the Presbyterians' pastor. The congregation couldn't be blamed that they hired a man with another steady job, but there was an attitude in the West, as Eunice (Mrs. Henry Ward) Beecher stated, "a clergyman's support was considered *charity,* and the small, very small amount *promised* was not always paid."

Proceed we to open the college.

For the growing state of Indiana, January 1825 marked the move of the capital from its deep south location in Corydon to a more centralized site, another river town planted on what was expected to be a navigable waterway. Because of the overabundance of forest, Hall fictionalized Indianapolis as "Timberopolis," another village of tall trees, logs, and stumps on White River.

In 1825, James Montgomery Higgins Allison was the Spencer, Indiana postmaster, with the official U.S. mail distribution point in his home. "Reader," writes Hall, "do you ever go the post-office?" He left on a September morning for Spencer, expecting for a long time a letter from Princeton. Calling James "Josey Jackson," Hall describes a bureau in Josey's back room,

> ...of which two drawers were Uncle Sam's Cabinet, the top drawer for *living* letters, the second (descending) for *dead* ones...the mail—if such may be called a dirty, famished, flapping scrawny pair of little saddlebags, containing three or four letters in one end, and half a dozen newspapers in the other—the mail came regularly (in theory) once a *month*, till the Hon. J. Young exerted himself in favour of his constituents, and then it came very irregularly once in *two weeks*. Sometimes there was an entire failure in the saddlebags' arrival. And this was occasioned by the clerk at

the Bloomington office who, whenever he discovered no letters for Spencer, retained the papers for private edification and to be forwarded next mail; at least our post-master Josey Jackson said so.

No explanation was given for the expected letter; it could have been a recommendation or a record of Hall's matriculation for the seminary board, a personal letter from a former instructor or friend. The non-condensed version of this postal encounter rings with the clear sound of truth!

In his storytelling, Baynard Hall may have been "almost literally true" in everything he wrote, but his deliberate jumble of time and his unintentional forgetfulness make it virtually impossible to outline events in strict chronological terms. Perhaps spitefully, he records the opening of the seminary as "the first day of May, at 9 1/2 o'clock. A.M., Anno Domini 1800 and so forth" in the 1843 edition of The New Purchase, and makes no changes in the 1855 revision. Because of fires at the university, to this day there is disagreement as to whether the college opened in 1824 or 1825, but if the seminary's newspaper advertisement is the more reliable source, the classes began April 4. Unfortunately, priceless and irretrievable information burned.

The January 1825 issues of the *Indiana Gazette* published in Bloomington carry a display ad running through April announcing that the seminary buildings are "now in a state of preparation" and will be ready for students by the first Monday of

April when the first session will begin under the superintendence of the "Rev'd. Baynard R. Hall whom the trustees have engaged as a teacher." While six trustees sign the advertisement, it surely was made up by Baynard Hall, or by the trustees, consulting with the newly hired instructor. Editors of newspapers in Indiana or other states were requested to give the ad at least a few insertions. Glowing in its description of Hall, the ad reads:

> Mr. Hall is a gentleman, whose classical attainments are perhaps not inferior to any in the western country; and whose acquaintance with the most approved methods of instruction in some of the best universities in the U. States, and whose morals, manners, and address render him every way qualified to give dignity and character to the institution.

As to the two buildings, the "big college" and the instructor's house, the advertisement stated they,

> ...are erected on an elevated situation, affording a handsome view of Bloomington the county seat...and also a commanding prospect of the adjacent country which is altogether pleasant and well calculated for rural retreats; and as it regards the healthiness of its situation, we hazard nothing in the assertion, that it cannot be excelled by any in the western country.

So far, the seminary had few rivals in regards its

claims. Admission fees were $2.50 per session with a year's tuition a total of $5.00. Good boarding was advertised as available with respectable families either in town or country at convenient distances and on "moderate terms, not exceeding a dollar and twenty-five cents per week." The two yearly sessions would amount to five months each. For five and six hours a day in the recitation room, and what other duties he performed as the only faculty and administrator, Hall received a beginning salary of $250.00 per year.

The institution for the time being was to be strictly classical and each scholar was expected to furnish his own supply of classical books, Latin and Greek texts with Hall's beloved *Virgil*, and no one was to bring along any English translations except those editions containing notes in English which were preferable for beginners. Students would be in classes and use textbooks that would be determined by "different degrees of improvement."

Hall writes of the opening day, "Boys and *young gentlemen,*" he addressed about 10 of the hopefuls remaining after interrogations,

> I am happy to see you; and we are now about to commence our State College, or as some call it, the Seminary. I hope all feel what an honour attends being the first students in an institution so well endowed; and which, therefore, by proper exertions on your parts, may eventually rise to the level of eastern

colleges and become a blessing to
our State and country. You have all, I
suppose, procured the necessary books,
of which notice was given....

Among the responses came what can be deemed
the general expectations of those families who sent
their boys off for higher learning:

Mr. Hall, I fotch'd my copy-book and
a bottle of red-ink to sit down siferin in,
and daddy wants me to larn bookeepin
and surveyin.

"There is," wrote Hall, "a misunderstanding with
some, both as to the books and the whole design
and plan of the school I perceive." Boys and young
gentlemen they were: Samuel Campbell Dunn, 16;
his brother James Wilson Dunn, 18; William McKee
Dunn, another brother, would enter the next term
at age 11. Their first cousin, James A. Maxwell, was
13. The others who were older "young gentlemen"
were in their late teens or early twenties.

The scene was set early for misunderstandings
and resentment between the college and the town,
and onto this stage would walk, literally because
he traveled from Ohio on foot, another instructor,
he of math and scientific things and Presbyterian
persuasion, John Harney, who would add fuel to
the coming controversy. But before the advent of
a teaching partner, the Halls experienced again the
pain of parting.

Chapter 12

My mother-in-law had been a very beautiful woman.

In January 1826, Ann Young and Martha Doughty each sold 80 acres to Elisha McGinnis, for which the sisters each received $250.00. On the 15th of January, Isaac Reed preached his last sermon at Bethany Church and wrote that he did not know what the little church would do.

In March, Ann moved into the Reed cabin. On the eighth she asked that a communion service be held. Bethany church members were called and her pastor sons-in-law who regarded her with tender respect were present for a "most solemn and tender communion meeting. The text was Luke 2:29, 30, 'Lord now lettest thou thy servant depart in peace...' From this time, she still gradually declined."

Hall recalled,

She was too pious, too humble

and meek, and childlike ever to think her lovely temper, resigned spirit, and disinterested goodness to be, as they were, a bright and burning light. In early life she was said to be surpassingly beautiful. But danger and temptation from beauty were soon prevented; in the midst of her bloom her enchanting face was forever marred by the fearful traces of small-pox. Yet in spite of this, and even in advanced life, rare was it to behold a countenance more agreeable than hers...her person was tall and finely proportioned and so imposing her mien, from a native dignity of soul, that had her original beauty remained, Mrs. Young must have always appeared a Grace. She was well educated and extensively read in history and many other important secular subjects but her chief reading had always been that best of books, the Bible...She read one other book, Ambrose's *Looking Unto Jesus*, and these two books in the latter months of her life, owing to the nature of her disease, she read on her knees. This was ...an aneurysm of the femoral artery of long continuance and towards the last exceedingly painful, and from which, from an early period of its existence had been pronounced fatal.

Isaac Reed wrote this tribute: "In the winter of

1825 –26 she was so feeble as to have to keep to her bed almost the whole time; her pains were nearly constant; her sufferings very great." On April 5, 1826, with her family present, "and upon the heads of each of her four little grandchildren she laid her feeble hands in token of her blessing and soon after breathed out her spirit."

Those children were Martha Doughty Reed, age five; Lydia Ann Lapsley Reed, three; Sarah Lewis Reed, seven months, and Elizabeth Hall, almost two years old. Ann died, Reed wrote, with reason clear and good hope.

> She believed the Divine promises and peace, the Saviour's benediction to his disciples, reigned in her soul.

> Thus in Christian faith and heavenly hope died Mrs. Ann Young at the Cottage of Peace in Owen County, Indiana, aged 63 years, 7 months, 9 days. Her funeral was held the second day after her death and an appropriate and solemn service preached at the house by the Rev. George Bush of Indianapolis.

It can be assumed that someone from the neighborhood rode to the capital to get Rev. Bush in anticipation of the need of his services.

They buried her near the tannery; no trace of her grave exists.

**I may look on trees planted in
company with others, but we shall
never sit together under their shade.**

Endings and beginnings mark the year of the
breaking up of the Young settlement. Likely John
Holmes and nephew John M. Young moved in
together because both remained in the vicinity
after the death of Ann Young and the departure
of the Halls and Reeds. For a time Aunt Doughty
remained in the settlement. There were trips back
and forth between the family in Owen County and
the family relocated in Monroe. One of those visits
was to serve as a farewell reunion when the Reeds
went away and Uncle Thomas Holmes and Aunt
Nancy left to build a cabin somewhere on Lake
Michigan.

In May 1826, Isaac and Elinor with three
youngsters aboard left in their "wheeled carriage"
for a wet, dreary, and tedious journey to New York
where he had relatives Elinor had never met and
where a church in Moriah called him as its minister.
Hall remembered,

> We took a mournful farewell of the
> two families going from the settlement
> and with no expectation of ever meeting
> again in this life. True, some of these
> persons, wanderers like ourselves, we
> did meet for a brief space in other parts
> of the United States again; but others
> we have never seen since the morning of
> our separation.

The reference to Thomas and Nancy Holmes' departure was omitted in the 1855 edition.

The seminary trustees placed another insertion of an advertisement in the *Indiana Gazette* running from March 30, again asking editors of other newspapers to allow some space for the ad. The text read: "Notice The Spring session of the STATE SEMINARY OF INDIANA, for the Second year will commence on Monday, the first day of May next." The fee, $2.50 per session, had not changed.

During the heat of summer, both young gentlemen and their 28-year-old instructor perspired and struggled through drills and recitations of languages foreign to their ears. If that southern dialect carried over into the student translators' speech, it can be imagined how *veni, vidi, vici* resounded in the hall of learning. With his flair for drama, the professor organized the Henodelphisterian Society, each member taking on a Greek or Roman name. Despite negative criticism from some former students in their mature years, it is difficult to believe a teacher with Hall's great humor, perception, and imagination to be a dull and uninspired mentor in the classroom.

In late July 1826, the *Bloomington Republican* published an announcement for Mary A. Hall and Martha M. Young, proposing to open in Bloomington,

> An Academy for Young Ladies on the first day of next December, under the direction of Mr. B.R. Hall, Principal

of the state seminary. At present the following parts only, of an useful and ornamental education, are comprised in the planning. Orography, Reading, Penmanship, Arithmetic, Grammar, Punctuation, Geography, Sacred and Profane History, Belles Lettres, including exercises in original composition and Needle-Work. If required, a class will be instructed in the Latin and Greek Language.

Should these classes warrant a sufficient enrollment of young women, the two sisters and their director would add Natural and Moral Philosophy, Chemistry, Astronomy, the Projection of Maps, Algebra, Euclid's Elements. Music and Drawing would require the employment of "other teachers and masters," the foregoing subjects being more than enough for the two and a half faculty. A lengthy list of rules, regulations and stipulations finished the advertisement and demonstrated the teaching staff seemed to know what they were doing. No student could be under 10 years of age and each scholar,

…must be able to spell words of three syllables and add with tolerable facility. Lessons for the most part must be learned at home, the whole morning from 9 o'clock until at noon will be spent in reciting and receiving instruction. The afternoon will be entirely devoted to Needle-Work.

To a community not that avidly engaged in promoting education for their children, it's highly likely a school for females was another factor in the charge that Hall and family were "big-bug aristocrats," and why would girls need to pay for instructions in sewing?

Facts and details about the endeavors of Mary Ann Hall and sister Martha Morris Young to conduct a school are not to be found. Hall's recounting of a trip north to escort girls home from school (in which he writes of visiting Tippecanoe Battlefield) and the girls helping decorate for a college exhibition are the minimal mentions in *The New Purchase.*

Autumn returned and the first day of the meeting of the newly formed Indiana Synod was held at Vincennes on October 18. Eight ministers including Hall and twelve ruling elders including Uncle John Holmes were present. Noticeably absent was the zealous Isaac Reed who would find the coming spring weather in upstate New York too taxing for his weak lungs.

Hall writes of the "ecclesiastical" trip to the "Big Meeting" through the course of four chapters.

While the Presbyterians were gathering at Vincennes, further up the Wabash and at the mouth of the Mississinewa River, the Potawatomi and Miami were negotiating treaties that would cede to the United States land that became a portion of the Michigan Road and a canal.

On December 31, 1826, by whose invitation

we are not told, Baynard R. Hall, Principal of the State Seminary, preached an evocative sermon to the Indiana General Assembly fitting for the end and beginning of a year titled, "Righteousness the Safeguard and Glory of a Nation."

He spoke:

The soldiers of the Revolution, like aged trees, are one after another, silently falling around us. The ancient senators, and fathers, and sages, are going down fast into the grave. The old pillars of the republic are gradually mouldering into ruins, the stars are descending beneath the horizon. For two of these, Jefferson and Adams, we recently wore the sackcloth of mourning.

Six months earlier on July 4, Thomas Jefferson and John Adams passed into glory, each thinking the other survived.

Hall concluded: *This republic with all its unspeakable blessings, the reward of the noble exertions of the mighty dead is ours; but yours, in a great measure is it to say, senators and representatives, governors and judges, whether it shall belong to posterity. To you is it now committed; you have solemnly sworn to guard it: that oath is registered in heaven. I charge you all then, by the blood of slain warriors; by the toil of our fathers; by your plighted faith; I charge you by all the blessings of liberty and by all the curses of slavery; by all the hopes of the present and the interests of future millions: I charge you by the approbation of a patriot's conscience, and by the remorse of the dying traitor; I charge you by the fearful bar of the eternal God...that you strive in every possible way, but chiefly by your personal holiness, faith in Christ, and prayer to the throne of grace, to promote the righteousness of this, our independent and blessed country.*

In this almost 23-page sermon, the preacher reminded the public servants, "As every person constitutes part of a people, so his conduct goes toward the forming of national character."

And maybe sometime in this year of endings and beginnings, a member of the Young settlement family dropped a brand-new half dollar. Farmer Robert Bonness noticed a disc-shaped form in the soil of his bean field, alighted from his tractor, and wiped away a possible 156 years of dust from the coin in 1982.

Chapter 13

...in the pell-mell style of history...

An increase in salary to $400.00 a year was a vote of confidence in the professorship of Baynard Rush Hall in 1827 and "for the good of the people general" the trustees resolved to elect a professor of mathematics. Hall wrote,

> ...this enraged the people who set no value on learning and deemed one small salary a waste of the poor people's education money, but when rumor declared we intended to elect a man nominally a Rat, the wrath was roused of the people, religious, and irreligious, of all other sects...the people having united the peoples in a fixed purpose, viz.—to keep out a Rat, but not having united them in any purpose of putting in anybody else, the people, now sovereign and of many kings, held a meeting up

town in the courthouse yard; while we, the trustee-people and sovereigns of another sort, were holding our meeting to elect a professor in the prayer-hall of Big College.

"Rats," the euphemism for Presbyterians, was a popular term in the growing division between town and gown.

Under the leadership of county clerk, deputy postmaster, town librarian, and brother of Enos Lowe of Big Fire exhumation, Jacob B. Lowe, came a "formidable battalion into the meeting to give us our orders," and to inform the trustees, et al. that "they have no right to give away their edicashion money without the people's consent" and among other arguments protested "they did not want two teachers of the same religion!" David Maxwell established some order to the chaos and at the word "adjourned," ending Dr. Maxwell's speech came a violent and simultaneous rush...with some of the malcontents attempting to seize and destroy the clerk's record. Jacob Lowe came by his antagonism honestly; his father William was not in the Presbyterian camp either. That semi-riot ended but the roiling opposition did not. The protesters were too late; the trustees had hired their choice, and now there was another fly in the community's ointment. Petitions charging sectarianism would pass from communities to the legislature for many sessions to come; they were ignored.

Dr. Maxwell, beleaguered by charges of

sectarianism, was forced to address a long editorial to the people of Monroe County in May 1825, stating he returned from legislative duties to learn there were rumors circulating in his district that he had introduced a bill in the House of Representatives to establish the Presbyterian Church as the state church by law!

John Hopkins Harney, a Kentuckian graduating from Miami University in Oxford, Ohio in 1827, was available. He was a tough and independent young man, said to have walked from Ohio to Bloomington to start his teaching career at the Indiana Seminary. Harney lost his father in his youth and had been raised in the home of a cousin, Benjamin Mills, Judge of the Kentucky Appellate Court and law partner of Henry Clay. J.H. Harney was learned in the natural sciences as well as mathematics. In May 1827, he was the groom of Martha Rankin Wallace, said to be related to Lew Wallace, and maybe a half-or step-sister of the wife of John Young, thus having a kinship connection to Baynard Hall as well as being his colleague. Harney and Hall in the future found themselves aligned on the opposite side of two fences, the Rats facing some disgruntled students and one not-so-passive, aggressive college president.

While Hall dated a trip to Tippecanoe Battlefield as 12 years after the 1811 conflict, more than likely it was during the first year that his sister-in-law Martha M. Young, assisted perhaps part-time by Mary Ann Hall, was engaged in teaching young women. He devoted three chapters in telling of the escorting of seven of the academy girls to their homes in the north, one or two near Lafayette, Indiana—a father, a brother and an additional male on the trip; 11 people were carried by 10 horses. The father and brother were Williamson Dunn, his son, and daughter Mary, all then of Crawfordsville. Another student was Charille Durkee, daughter of a Lafayette physician. The young ladies of Miss Martha Young's Bloomington Female Academy were called "Hoosierinas" in the 1855 edition of *The New Purchase.*

> I do wish you could have seen us set out...the clapping on of horse-blankets and saddles, male and female...what a drawing of girths! What a fixing and unfixing and refixing of saddle-bags. Then the girls...they seemed to be everywhere at once—up stairs, down stairs, on the stairs, in the closet under the stairs!

After depositing the girls at their various homes, an adventure that used up a week, he and two young men rode on to the Tippecanoe battlefield. Somberly he walked the site of the 1811 battle observing even then some scattered remains.

> We lingered at Tippecanoe till the latest possible moment; there was, in the wildness of the battlefield—in my intimate acquaintance with some of its actors—in the living trees, scarred and hacked with bullet and hatchet and

marked with names of the dead—in the
wind so sad and melancholy—something
so like embodied trances, that I wandered
the field all over....

Included in the detailed account of the
experience is a poem dedicated to the memory
of Joseph Daviess, one of nine killed in the battle
whose surnames were attached to new Indiana
counties. Why he gave this particular attention to
Daviess is not clear, but most certainly in Owen and
Monroe counties there were veterans with whom
he could have had an acquaintance and friendship.

Hall observed a burial.

...our windings...brought us to a sight
mournful and solemn—a coffin in which
rested an Indian babe. This rude coffin
was supported in the crotch of a large
tree, and secured from being displaced
by the wind, being only a rough trough
dug out with a tomahawk and in which
was deposited the little one, and having
another similar trough bound down over
the body with strips of pawpaw. Sad
seemed the dreamless sleep of the poor
innocent so separate from the graves of
its fathers and the children of its people.
Mournful the voice of leaves whispering
over the dead in that sacred tree. The
rattling of naked branches there in the
hoarse winds of winter—how desolate...
yet if one after death *could* lie amid

thick and spicy evergreen branches near
the dear friends left—instead of being
locked in the damp vault or trodden like
clay in the deep, deep grave...but would
that be rebellion against the sentence
"dust thou art, and unto dust shalt thou
return"? —then let our bodies be laid in
the silence and the dark till the morning
and the life.

What must have seemed a Godsend to Hall
occurred when the president of Miami University
recommended in May 1827 an honorary master's
degree be awarded the Hoosier professor.

In Moriah, New York, Isaac Reed was
negotiating with a publisher for his little journal
titled *The Christian Traveler.* During the last month
of Elinor's fifth pregnancy, Isaac coughed blood.
The Reeds surely wrote their relatives of the birth
of their first son George Whitefield "Whit" Reed
born June 25. The Halls had another daughter born
late in 1827 or early 1828, a baby whose name was
never mentioned in his writing.

...the glory of Young settlement was fading.

At Gosport flatboats embarked for the White
River leg of trips to the Ohio River and New
Orleans, and John M. Young, bachelor merchant,
accountant, and land dealer, became a candidate for
the legislature; his brother-in-law, Professor Hall,
was happy to go campaigning with him, to assist

in speechifying, and generally observe the political scene in early Indiana.

The price of liberty, eternal vigilance, is well paid in a New Purchase. With us it was watched by all classes, and throughout the year; it was indeed the universal business. Our offices all, from Governor down to a deputy constable's deputy and fence-viewer's clerk's first assistant, were in the direct gift of the people. We even elected magistrates, clerks of court, and the judges presiding and associate! And some who knew better, yet for rabble rousing purposes, gravely contended that trustees of colleges, and all presidents, professors, and teachers should be elected directly by the people. Our social state therefore was forever in ferment...and everybody expected at some time to be a candidate for something; or that his uncle would be; or his cousin, or his cousin's wife's cousin's friend...so that everybody and everybody's relations and everybody's relations' friends were forever electioneering....

Because John M. Young was a jolly good fellow, and had obviously won the respect and trust of the voting men in Spencer and Gosport, points in between and around, and downriver in Greene County, he was duly elected by a majority of 171

votes and, came the 1828 session of the Indiana
General Assembly, he took his seat among the
representatives to speak for the constituents of
two counties. By an act of January 24, 1828, four
days before Baynard's 30th birthday, the seminary
graduated to college status; Hall became professor
of ancient languages and no longer Principal.

On May 7, Hall sent a letter to Andrew Wylie,
President of Western Pennsylvania's Washington
College and a candidate for the Indiana office,
extolling the healthy climate of the Bloomington
area, noting the small number of deaths, but
mentioning that he had buried an infant daughter,
dead of a "peculiar eruption."

Isaac Reed and family returned to Bloomington,
and another child was born to the Halls. He was
named Rush Baynard. He was the second son and
fifth of their children, the only one to bear the name
Rush.

Visits from the family remaining in Owen
County continued. In Bloomington, Hall wrote,

> ...my emotions became most
> delightful whenever returning on
> Saturday evenings from a short squirrel
> hunt, I discerned at a distance Uncle
> John's horse tied to our rack. Often
> too, would some of us, the day he was
> expected, sit the last hour at an upper
> window and watch the leafy barrier
> where our dear friend was expected
> momentarily to break through into the

mellow light of the departing sun...that dear old man was so loved, we felt like hugging and kissing the very horse that brought him.

A Christmas crisis occurred when the family in Bloomington waited for the arrival of Uncle John, Aunt Doughty and John M. Young.

For this visit, our whole house had been prepared—bedrooms were arranged to render sleeping warm and refreshing—fat poultry was killed—mince pies concocted, cider bought; in short, all the goodies, vegetable, animal, and saccharine, usually congregated at this joyous season, were stored and ready. In the parlour, a compound of sitting-room, dining-room and bed-chamber, a magnificent fire of clean white sugar-tree with a green beech back-log was warming and enlivening; while the lid of the piano was raised with copies of favourite pieces ready, and an eight-keyed flute and a four-stringed violin on its top—all ready for a grand burst of fun and frolic at the coming of loved ones.

When hours passed and "it was so very much later than our old folks had been wont to come, we all sat now in the gloom of disappointment...uneasy, with forebodings of evil, when the clatter of a horse moving rapidly over the frozen earth called us in haste to the door." John Young had come for the doctor and stopped to tell the family that Uncle John had fallen the day before and broken the head of a femur, falling at the door of the stable. Because John Young was delayed in getting home, Aunt Doughty tried to drag Uncle John on a buffalo robe into the cabin and was only able to do so by the aid of a passing neighbor. Aunt Doughty "forced the leg into something like a natural position, splinted and bandaged the leg to the best of her ability." One of Dr. Maxwell's students in his absence came to attend the patient, but was satisfied with Aunt Doughty's efforts.

After 70 days in bed, Uncle John rose with a two-inch deficit in his right side and "yet, so youthful and buoyant the spirit of this noble old gentleman, that he and I hunted often together after his recovery— he walking with a crutch in one hand and a heavy rifle in the other." This accident and the dreariness of cabin life for the old people, and the risk of death from the absence of ordinary help prompted the sale of the tannery. It seems most probable that Uncle John stayed near John M., both being in the 1830 Owen County census. But Aunt Doughty came to Bloomington, able to divide her time between the Halls and the Reeds, being great-aunt Doughty to a growing extended family.

In February 1829, John Young signed a deed to sell acreage with the exception of a 10-feet square plot...where rests, Hall wrote in 1842, "...far from us, scattered as we are, and ever in this life shall be, the ashes of the mother." After the last of the settlement land was sold, Hall only passed that way once, ever after avoiding a new road that passed between the cabins and that went by the empty grave of Big Fire.

Yet, while all the changes were for the better...I sat on my horse and had one of my girlish fits of tears! Yes—I cried like Homer's heroes—and that in spite of the critic, who running over the book to make an article, will say, "the author, tender-hearted soul, cries again towards the close of...Chap. xii. p. 318."

Yes! I cried!

Chapter 14

...is it any wonder Calvinism is on the decline?

When Hall met with illustrator William Momberger in 1855, he discussed a drawing of an African American preacher at a camp meeting, and it is one of the illustrations that the artist produced (three pictures for $70) for the revised edition of *The New Purchase*. The preacher was Aaron Wallace of the area's few black families. As Rev. Mizraim Ham, the character's discourse on David and Goliath was raw and broad parody: "The Fillystines they had thar army up thar on a mounting, and King Sol he had hissin over thar, like, across a branch, amoss like that a one thar—and it was chuck full of sling rock all along the bottom." The camp, Hall wrote, was an old and favorite ground, eight miles from Bloomington; it had been the theater for "many a spirit-stirring drama," and "many a harvest of glory reaped in battling with the 'devil and his legions.'"

Wise Congress! Making no laws establishing religion or prohibiting its free exercise was justified; what legislation could have managed the religious pluralism that even in The Purchase was dividing folks into Methodists and Baptists, Old and New School and other Presbyterians, New Lights, and Disciples of Christ, and etceteras, and that was just the beginning of independent Hoosiers choosing to shop for denominations and non-denominations and all their splinters.

Why, the Reverend Hall wrote,

…whole families should once or twice a year break up for two weeks; desert domestic altars; shut up regular churches; and take away children from school; why cook lots of food at extra trouble and ill-bestowed expense; why rush to the woods and live in tents, with peril to health and very often ultimately with loss of life to feeble persons; why folks should do these and other things under a belief that the Christian God is a God of the woods and not of the towns, of the tents and not of the churches, of the same people in a large and disorderly crowd and not in one hundred separate and orderly congregations—why? why? I had in my simplicity repeatedly asked and received for answer: Oh! Come and see! And because he had often refused to attend, and "it being often said, 'yes,—

Hall's an honest sort of man, but why
don't he go out to camp and git religion?'
I determined now to go.

Confessing that his portrayal and critiques of
the camp meeting were a composite of all he had
witnessed, Baynard observed from a somewhat
skewed position as a stalwart keeper of Old
School Presbyterian tenets and he viewed from a
biased stance the self-ordained soul-savers and
representatives of new denominations; but any
disinterested observer could have come away
with the same impressions. His caricatured tale
of camp meeting antics reflects gatherings at least
in 1824 and 1827, mixed with in-home sermons in
the primitive cabins of lay preachers. Those camp
meetings were the Kentucky style of gathering
which in fact were well-planned and were nearly
always interdenominational.

In September 1827, at Blue Spring in Monroe
County, Barton W. Stone, a former language
teacher and Presbyterian minister who left the
fold after sincere disagreement with some basics
of Presbyterianism, was present for the Indiana
Christian Conference. Among the ordained
preachers there was Joseph Berry. Where Rev. Hall
encountered Berry is uncertain, but Berry took a hit
in Hall's book in the person of "Doctor Lobelia." In
Lobelia's sermon, as reported by Baynard, educated
pastors are attacked:

> ...I never rub'd my back agin a collige,
> nor git no sheepskin and allow the Apos-

tuls didn't nithur.... And as to Sprightly's preachurs, don't they dress like big-bugs and go ridin around the Purchis on hunder-dollar hossis...we only wants beleevur's baptism...Aposotul's Christianity... when Christians...went down into the water and was buried in the gineine sort of baptism by emerzhin.

The theme of the camp meetings, in general Hall stressed, was spiritual warfare against Calvinism in any of its ways, shapes, or forms. Hall compared Barton Stone with "Peter Stone," a play on the Apostle Peter. Barton Stone had conducted meetings in the local courthouse and was not without a modicum of fame.

In the camp meeting story, Sprightly (the Hall-invented name for Rev. William Armstrong) rebuts Berry's sermon:

The pious brother took a great deal of time to tell what we soon found out ourselves—that he never went to college and don't understand logic. He boasts too of having no sheepskin to preach by; but I allow any sensible buck-sheep would have died powerful sorry if he'd ever thought his hide would come to be handled by some preachers.

Predestination came under fire in a humorous paragraph and for the whole story of the axing of certain long-held beliefs, it is for the learned theologians to enter this argument—and for the purists who would question the veracity of Hall's report, a full reading of the camp meeting chapter is advised with the reader bearing in mind Hall's lumping together various of his experiences and observations, not even omitting a knock-down, drag-out fight with Satan.

"A camp-meeting was, all things considered, the very best contrivance and means for making the largest number of converts in the shortest possible time...and also for enlarging most speedily the bounds of a Church Visible and Militant," he quipped in print. The fate of babies not baptized was not left untouched in this chapter. Rev. Armstrong was quoted as preaching free salvation for all, and a denial that God foreordained condemnation of those infants and children. "Sprightly" pounded home an anti-Calvinistic concept that "God did not *wish* to *foreknow some* things!"

As if to interject a sudden memory during the rambling course of writing *The New Purchase*, the father of little Elizabeth recorded a very short and sweet domestic incident:

Our family was usually very harmonious, yet the surface of our quiescence was occasionally ruffled. For instance, I believed that Miss Elizabeth Hall, now nearly four years old, if she *did* spell, ought to do it by sounds of the letters; Aunt Doughty insisted it ought to be in the march of mind way—by pictures of things. And Aunt Doughty carried the day, affirming that the baby could learn to spell in six days! I, not caring whether she spelled or not, provided she had plenty of air and sunshine and played all the time with a kitten or a doll...but when I persisted that the little one could not ever learn to *spell* by pictures, and must do it by the sounds of separate letters, away flounced Aunt Doughty after a caricature book; and then flouncing back she said with a voice of triumph: "There, spell her any where."

"Well, dearee, what does *c-o-w* spell?"—covering at the same time the figure with the hand.

"Cow," said the baby in an instant.

"There!—now sir!" says Aunt Doughty.

"How do you know, dearee, that it spells cow?" I asked.

"I sees the –legs!" replies the baby.

Dear one! That was true learning Aunt Doughty gave you daily from the Word of God. She did, indeed by her living voice, teach in figures about heaven! And it was to that heaven, dearest! you went...when death so strangely quenched the light of those sweetly soft blue eyes!

Perhaps this poignant memory emerged when Hall was ruminating disagreements of dogmas, doctrines and disciplines. He ended the little story of

Elizabeth by asking, "Parents, do you have children in heaven? The author hopes to have five."

By the 1855 edition, the author writes with no uncertainty at all that he has six children in heaven.

Chapter 15

...a fresh start would be given
in its growth.

Such were the high hopes for the shipping port
community on the bluff in Owen County where John
M. Young had relocated to live and store-keep, that
"if some folks did not look sharp," the Legislature
would move the college there, "or at least create
a branch College!" At the first sale of lots, Hall
reported, there was a flush of sales then after Young's
places were built and a few other buildings put up,
"the rage for improvement ceased." In 1828, a year
before the town of Gosport was platted, the site was
considered a prime location for a commercial center.
Like his guardian, Dr. Rush, who claimed to have
given Tom Paine the title, "Common Sense," Hall
claims to have suggested "Gosport" as the name of
the town with respect to the Goss family who were
early settlers. As his alias for the town, Hall called
it "Guzzleton" for reasons only guessed (historians

know that whiskey and spring water were the means of hydration, even after the digging of wells, in those times). Isaac Brasier, it was recorded, distilled fire water on his farm, making peach brandy and the best whiskey. Peaches and corn were processed on shares or exchanged for the final product at 15 and 20 cents per gallon at the Brasier place just north of Gosport and west of the Young settlement.

To give impetus to sales of lots and expansion of business, the forerunners of a Chamber of Commerce created the first community festival: "The Patroons...thought if a Fourth of July could be got up and the place become a centre for stump-speeching, electioneering, horse-jockeying and other democratical excellences...", the town could go from "Little Guzzleton" to "Great Guzzleton."

"Hence...there was to be a grand Barbecue, with the reading of the Declaration of Independence, and great speeches from Baynard Hall of Bloomington and other fellow-citizens!" Hall and colleague John Harney visited on the third to witness arrangements, "and as such an affair may be novel to some, we shall confine ourselves to that, taking for granted most have once or twice heard the Declaration and also the patriotic orations of the season." The site of the festivities was on a plateau below the bluff and yet overlooking the river. One hundred yards by 50, "it was covered with fine and luxuriant grass, usually cropped by cows and horses, but now smoothly and evenly mown with scythes." Shade was provided by hackberry, buckeye, sycamore and other trees and

...near the center of this sylvan salon was set the table, one-hundred and fifty feet long, two-inch planks in double layers, resting every ten feet on horizontal pieces of saplings which in turn were supported by strong forked saplings planted several feet in the earth. Neither nail of iron, nor peg of wood, confined the planks—they reposed by their own gravity. On each side of the table, at ten feet distant and at intervals of five feet, were planted in the earth small trees with all their green and branching tops...forced together and tied with bark-twines over the table.

Sitting on seats low enough that "our mouths be as near the food as possible—so that if the legs were judiciously disposed under the table and the head properly inclined above, the contents of one's plate could be shoveled into the masticating aperture with amazing dexterity and grace." The diners consumed boiled hams, pones, pies, tarts, sorrel and Irish potato pies brought by the women, and the "beasts and birds" barbecued in a trench 20 feet long , four wide and three deep, all this under a shady arcade.

The Fourth's celebration began with the firing off of cannons made by boring logs with a two-inch auger—the "Hoosier artillery," Hall observed, "made a very reasonable noise considering they could rarely be fired more than once, being

wonderfully addicted to bursting!" Then there was
what must have been the genesis of July 4 parades
in the far west. Three beech-cannons were fired,
burst, and signaled the procession on the cliff and
in the "center" of town, as it were, and men and
women alike (Hall notes "true woodsmen wish their
ladies to share in all that is pleasant and patriotic")
led by drum and fife and with pocket-handkerchief
flags flying, the "leading" citizens who were to read
and speak took up the line of march followed by
the,

> ...common and uncommon citizens,
> then certain independent ladies; and then
> young ladies with escorts, then the boys,
> then finally the rabble. After showing
> ourselves in the woods and bushes along
> the future streets of Great Guzzleton,
> and passing the store, tannery, the two
> cabins, we descended the cliff and
> marched to the speakers' scaffold to the
> tune of Yankee Doodle—or something
> tolerably like it...

Before the climax of the day, the "band" had
also played "Love and Sausages."

> We may not recount our jokes
> and raillery, and tilting of tables, and
> sinking of seats and spilling of gravy and
> upsetting of water.... But never was more
> good humour! Never heartier fellowship!
> No drunkenness...no profanity...no
> breaking of wine glasses—no singing of

nasty songs—no smoking of cigars—no genteel and polished doings at all. We were then too far West for refinements. And what did all that cost? Cost! Why nothing in the sense you mean. All was a contribution—a gift—and everybody did it; and everybody ate and drank that was invited and everybody that was *not* invited!

Notwithstanding the continuous feasting of many hundreds for four or five hours, large quantities—nay *heaps* of provisions were left; and...these in the spirit of *native* western hospitality were divided among the poorer of guests who carried away with them food enough for a week. And dear reader, out there the noble Declaration of Independence itself, when properly read and commented on as today by John Morris Young has an effect on backwoodsmen such as is rarely felt *now* in here.

Hall then named two of his Bloomington and two of his Owen County friends. "If you could have seen them...rise at one or two places and clench their rifles convulsively and with tearful eyes and quivering lips stand intently gazing on the face of that reader... Oh, could you have heard the enthusiastic cries, at the close, that came warm bursting from the very hearts of our congregation, men and women and children—"

As Hall ended the chapter about the Guzzleton barbecue on the Fourth of July, he nostalgically sighed for "that sylvan life," but never mentioned if at the reading of the names of those 56 Signers of the Declaration of Independence, his thoughts might have wandered to Dr. Benjamin Rush who risked his very life, his future, his family and his fortune when he affixed his signature to the sacred document.

Chapter 16

The society of Bloomington was not yet as refined as it might have been.

Indiana continued to grow from the bottom up. The people in Professor Hall's bailiwick who began to consider the importance of book learning took a short look at theories of education and came down on the side of *practical* education. "Useful, practical stuff." And why not; communities were works in progress and needed craftsmen and trades people, merchants, and farmers, smiths, surveyors, and a doctor and lawyer or two. Hence Hall's "discipline makes men" (and gentlemen), and "the proper foundation of the proper union of classical and abstract mathematical studies" came bump up against the learning of Latin solely for the understanding of legal terms, and students who were sorely lacking in the rudiments of the three R's and "jogerfree."

It was Baynard Hall's contention that a focus on educating for life as "mere western or eastern citizens," was discriminatory and that the best *intellectual* education, "paid for by the government" ought not to have exclusive regard to any class, any one art, trade, or profession, but should be given to the poor and the rich and equip for life in the world! A life that meant a lifetime of learning. He noted in no uncertain terms that the promotion of the college for some was only an inventive to boost the town's economy. "Only show that a school, an academy, a college, or a *church* will advance the value of town lots—bring in more consumers, create a demand for beef, cloth, pepper and salt, powder and shot; then from the vulgar plebeian dealing in shoe leather, up to the American *nobleman* dealing in shops and who retails butter and eggs, we shall hear one spontaneous voice in favor!"

The two-member faculty and the board, being after all realists, decided that since the state was expanding and there were potential students in new households, so should the institution increase its offerings, and thus the wooing of Andrew Wylie as the first official president got underway.

The first family event of the year 1829 was the birth of Elinor Catharine Reed, another daughter for Elinor and Isaac in January. In the months before the birth, both Isaac and Elinor had to recover from bouts of the recurring ailment that confined them in the same house, but apart, with treatment by Dr. Maxwell. The next cause for celebration was the

Baynard Rush Hall from the 1916 Princeton
edition of *The New Purchase*.

Isaac Reed, from portrait painted by
William S. Shackleford.

The Patriarchal Cabin

(Kitchen Cabin is 30 feet away)

E
<<< N S
W

XXXXXXXXXX XXXXXXXXXXXXX	Fireplace	XXXXXXXXXX XXXXXXXXXXXXX
Carlton's Study	Table	Parlor		Table	Ladies Private Room
		Potato Hole 20 bushels (under floor)			

(All above "rooms" are East of the Scotch Wall, hung over stout pole.) (This is the "honest" Scotch Wall Carpet with woolen side facing away from Parlor.)

Mr. and Mrs. Carlton's Room (on north of Grand Hall)	Stranger's Hospitality Room	Grand Hall 18 inches wide from front door to parlor	Very Small Room for Help	Widow Ladies & Miss Emily (trundle bed)	Uncle John & Nephew Room
			Toilette and Pantry	P E T T I C O A T S	
Inside length 17 ft 1 in. Exterior length 19 ft 2 in.			Window 4 panes 8x10		
XXXXXXXXXX	Front Door		XXXXXXXXXXXXXXXXXXX		

See page 94, 95 in James A. Woodburn's edition of *The New Purchase* Princeton University Press 1916.

Barton E. Richardson

The patriarchal cabin, as it might have been.

A view of part of the Young Settlement land
in Owen County, Indiana.

Momberger's illustration for
"Hunting Shirt Andy," 1855.

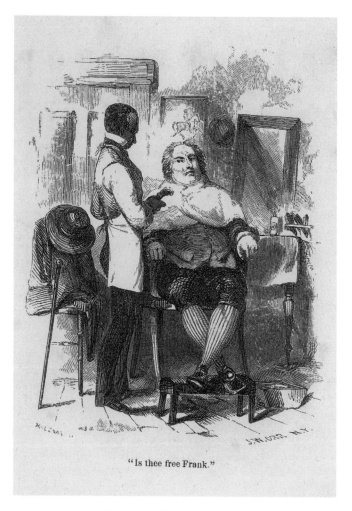

"Is thee free Frank."

Rush B. Hall's illustration for
Frank Freeman's Barber Shop, 1852.

Family graves, Cemetery of the Evergreens,
Brooklyn, New York: Holmes Hall,
Aunt Doughty, Carolina Hall, Baynard
and Mary Ann Hall, Martha Morris Young,
Edistina Hall, Rush Hall.

The Hall frame home in Brooklyn
became a row house.

wedding of 31-year-old bachelor John M. Young and a somewhat younger Aletha Wallace, two days after Rev. Baynard Hall baptized baby Elinor.

The wedding promoted buying and selling "broadcloth and trimmings, and silks, and satins—in short, all things for wedding suits, dresses and decorations and every mantua-maker, milliner, tailor, and shoemaker was in immediate requisition. Superfine flour, the best teas and coffees, the best loaf sugar, the best, in a word, of all persons and things from the beginning to the end of Bloomington... many articles were required from the Ohio River... so many messages were sent and so many packages brought by waggoners and travelers to and from, that long before the eventful day, half the State was advertised of the coming ceremony."

It increased borrowing and lending; "many who 'allowed' they would be asked had agreed to lend one another suitable apparel, from caps and curls upwards, to shoes and stockings downwards, and our bride's folks, not having domestic means enough, had borrowed far and wide every article in the shape of china, proper and mock, and silver, German and real. China and silver representatives were on that table of all the grand old-fashioned dignity once pertaining to the ancestry of Bloomington grandees, and whose pretensions to gentility thus shone forth..."

An eventful day it was. As the ceremony proceeded and the officiating minister Rev. Hall asked, *"pro formula,* if anyone present knows reason why the parties ought not to be united...if anybody inside answered, the voice was unheard in the horrid din from without that interrupted...," he recalled.

It is difficult to tell by Hall's account if the couple were duly wedlocked before the *Chevarai*, or shivaree as it is called in the vernacular to this day, erupted! "Two corn baskets full of cowbells tied to saplings—a score and a half of frying pans beat with mush sticks; two and thirty Dutch oven and skillet lids clashed as cymbals; fifty-three horse shoes played as triangles; ten large washtubs and seven small barrels drummed with fists and corncobs, one hundred and ninety-five quills prepared and blown as clarinets; forty-three tin whistles and baby trumpets blown till they all cracked; two small and one large military drums with six fifes, blown on D in alt, or thereabouts; add imitations of scalp and war cries...the *human* performers were estimated from two hundred and fifty to three hundred and fifty...."

To add to the pandemonium, through a window just behind the Owen girls, a 6-month-old, 50-pound pig was shoved into the room. While Hall's wryly embroidered facts and figures embellish the scene of the shivaree shambles, he surely did not fabricate the sudden discovery that his daughter Elizabeth, then about five, was bleeding from the nose and "went into fits from fright." He said in the conclusion that the retreat of the family from the wedding site was unimpeded and that "the spirit of frolic was up and aided by the spirit of the still." The wedding guests, those asked and those who infringed on hospitality, were into a melee that Dr. Maxwell, with the aid of those rustic friends Peter Batterton and James Borland, had to quell. "Rising in their majesty, the two men, despite the fact two or more schoolmasters were present, prevented violence and bloodshed; though destitute of learning and gravity, they were full of courage, manly feeling and muscular power!" Virginia and Kentucky blood ran hot, the pastor recalled.

The May 6, 1829 union of John Morris Young and his bride Aletha survived this tumultuous beginning but ended in divorce. It had been a speedy courtship, Hall said, and on John's side an affair of the heart. "Not I fear on hers. He certainly married not for *money.*" At the time of that writing, Hall believed she was dead. References to Aletha Wallace Young were omitted in the 1855 edition of *The New Purchase.*

Those academics and historians who were so sure that Baynard Hall wished to be the president of the college disregarded his statement that he was aware of his youth. Both Hall and Harney would have to admit to inexperience; they were in their first positions as full-time educators. Hall was 30 in 1828; Harney, 22. Wylie was 38 and had been the chief administrator of two colleges. Hall never directly indicated a desire to be the college president even though he may have been flattering himself to mention others thought him capable. His future would be in private schools where control of methods and curriculum was in his hands, but at the time and place of the Indiana Seminary, it is difficult to imagine the easy-going, jovial, squirrel-hunting lover of ancient languages, the outdoors, and cracker-barrel conversations to be tied down with the duties the president's office requires; but if he had hopes to lead the college, no fault should be laid at his doorstep for honest ambition. He wrote of his "wish to remain in a subordinate post to perfect himself in his favorite studies—languages, and history, and mathematics," insisting that "good professors were as important as a good president." Indeed.

Chapter 17

...we will esteem learning and discipline next to religion.

As the instructors Hall and Harney clung to their fixed models of education, and salaried at $400.00 a year each, they were still enthusiastically in favor of the appointment of Dr. Wylie. Baynard wrote in a letter to the candidate, "I do think, Sir, that the finger of Providence directs your path towards this place..." and continued on to say that he feared the ruin of the College of Indiana if Wylie declined the offer. Promising that he and Harney would stay, he advised, "your faculty desire you to have the principal hand." Harney, writing that the number of students had increased by 10 each session to 40, stressed in his assurance to Wylie that the board was composed of "men of the best talents...the management of the college however will be according to your own direction should you consent to be our president." A number of letters passed back and forth, including

Dr. Maxwell's, and in all from Bloomington there was an urgency and positive anticipation regarding the addition of a president. Wylie took his indecision to friend William McGuffey of the famed and long-used textbooks, and other advisors, and then agreed to accept the position. He dislodged his wife and family from comfortable and settled surroundings and moved to a society that would take some getting used to, a community described by Dr. Maxwell as not to be charged either with rudeness, nor refinement.

According to Baynard Hall, he, John Harney and Dr. David Maxwell stood the expense of the trip to the Ohio River to escort the Wylies from Louisville up to Bloomington. At the riverboat landing, Hall wrote, "the steamer was now seen descending on the swollen bosom of the waters, belching fire and smoke as if in labour and longing to be delivered of the great weight of character and influence she was painfully bearing to our inland wilds..."

On the 95-mile ride home, gregarious Hall with his buoyant personality and lively curiosity, "resolved to make the inland journey pleasant," and surely wishing to familiarize the president, "told about Bloomington and all the peoples, and trustees, and...all!" Admitting it was indiscreet, he wrote that he felt then like a son with a father. Wylie was interested in all this in-house information, and in "the leaky state of our mind...indeed...he started fresh leaks in a vessel that never held well at the best..." And so much of the gossip and small talk and revelations, and yes, opinions spilled by Hall were later to be regretted. "Twelve months after this ride, the Doctor did remember...all," and had used it with students, trustees, and townspeople. Hall in retrospect recalled that certain "brethren" had warned that Wylie was "no safe confidant and we should in the end find a person that could blow hot and cold with the same breath." But that was at a future time and on the trek back to Bloomington, Hall was happily thinking of the "rapid and lasting growth of learning, and science and civilization and religion." He mused that John Harney also rejoiced at the rebirth and almost guarantee that the college would thrive and prosper.

The gala welcoming for the new president and his family was to include an "illumination" of the college buildings. Mary Ann Hall and a dozen other women prepared the president's house and had a meal waiting.

As the presidential party neared Bloomington on the night of the arrival, they saw the college buildings were "tastefully illuminated in the eastern way, but on Biggest College, the new building under construction, poles with a bar had been erected with three candles representing the new leader and two professors. The students stood with a circle of candles below. It was a proud night! And not undelightful our emotions and anticipations as we stood in the edge of the wilderness, where lately only Indians had lived...and gazed on those symbolical tapers. But even while we gazed, those tapers became oddly extinguished! First one after another died away the lights of the circle!—then the lights at the extreme ends of the bar, first Hall's, then Harney's—while the light topping the pole was left, feebly burning indeed, and spluttering, yet triumphant and alone! Was that ominous what follows?" Aunt Doughty insisted it was so; she had had a dream that very night in which Baynard was "seated in his great rocking chair on top of Biggest College, and that a wind, insidious, noiseless and yet resistless, came like a double-blowing tornado, and hurled him to the earth!"

To the chagrin of those in town who grumbled "sectarianism," another Presbyterian pastor, another Pennsylvanian aristocrat had joined the college ranks. But on the October day when Dr. Maxwell presented the keys to the college to Dr. Wylie, the courthouse was packed by an audience who heard "Of What Advantage is a College to the Community?" Spoken from an educator's point of view, Wylie's address probably evoked no adverse criticism from Professor Hall. Assuming his post, Wylie extended the class structure and curriculum, adding junior and senior classes and new and broader courses, a more demanding row for young men to hoe. The new program opened in December 1829. Of necessity, Wylie became an instructor; Hall and Harney continued classical languages and mathematics among other duties. Wylie instituted his modes and methods and the college no longer looked on the brink of failure. For a time Hall and

Wylie seemed to have set aside their opposing views of what makes a Presbyterian; Wylie and Harney had not let mutual antagonism get the better of them, yet Baynard Hall began to feel their leader was treating his faculty as no more than "ushers."

James Borland, agent of the seminary as board treasurer, transferred ownership of part of lot 38 in the seminary addition to Baynard Hall and Martha Doughty for $248.00 on November 20, 1829. Theirs was a warm and harmonious home; Aunt Martha Doughty domiciled there when she was not sharing her homemaking skills with the Reeds or Uncle John or John Young and Aletha. Her namesake Martha Morris Young, the unmarried schoolmistress, was a household fixture at the Halls' residence and with little Elizabeth and Rush Baynard, all looked forward to the birth of another child. He was born the last week in May, and was named Baynard Chisholm Hall.

Four young men were handed diplomas in the first commencement of the Indiana College in 1830; young men who knew Greek and Latin and chose careers in law, medicine, the ministry, and government: James Dunn, James Rollins, Michael Hummer, and William Hamilton Stockwell. Isaac Reed hurried home from a synod meeting to attend the commencement exhibition.

Some will think we are manufacturing a character...

Because this is Baynard Rush Hall's biography,

there are bias and slant to be sure. The lasting legacy for good that Dr. Andrew Wylie's tenure provided can be read elsewhere. Professor Hall vented his rancor in the 1843 *New Purchase* but omitted most of it in the 1855 version. He had somewhat mellowed over time and sincerely regretted especially one chapter devoted to the man he had considered an enemy. From that particular chapter: "The president had contradicted the faculty in public on several occasions, and aimed to consider and treat them as boys...and he permitted some students to be graduated who held imperfect diplomas." To further his argument, Hall listed eight reasons not why the faculty disliked Wylie but whence came Wylie's dislike of the two-member faculty:

> ...his jealousy of equals and suspicious and untrustful temper; his determination for a very low grade of studies, especially in Mathematics and even in Classics—he being resolved to level down and not level up; his love of ease and wish to get along with a relaxed or rather no discipline; his using discipline as an instrument of avenging himself on students disliked by him; his domineering and tyrannical temper; his prying disposition, by which he was led to have spies in the professors' classes and to watch when they came and went to and from duties, etc., his desire to make room for former pupils and relatives.

And last but not the least to the Rev. Hall, "his erroneous theology."

The crowning thorn to any teacher might be when the man considered a colleague announced to a class in progress that should the professor in charge be unable to explain and instruct, his "deficiencies" would be rectified by the president if the student or students wished to visit his study.

Along with President Wylie came young men with backgrounds and perhaps agendas not conducive to fraternal camaraderie in the far west setting. Some disliked Hall whether for his teaching methods or his philosophy of discipline. In 1830, the Hall-founded Henodelphisterian Society was split by the withdrawal of those students.

Among the student body, Hall wrote, "generally the young men of a New Purchase are superior to the young gentlemen of the old settlements, in both scholarship and elocution." Citing as reasons, the New Purchasers saw learning as a novelty, had more energy, fewer temptations to idleness and dissipation, and considered the ten dollars a year tuition hard to obtain and not to be squandered—after all, ten dollars would buy nearly ten acres of land. Two students were memorialized by Hall: James Wilson Dunn, who possessed perseverance "to so great a degree as to make it a substitute for genius." Dunn from that tough pioneer Hoosier family "studied and re-wrote a composition thirty-six times." Joseph Albert Wright was a dirt poor boy, "even for the Purchase," Hall said. He lived hand to mouth and grubbed for every penny he could get for his education. Joseph spent two days in the woods, staying overnight, looking for Hall's wandering cow, spent days digging a waterless well, worked in the town library, rang the school bell and laid the fires.

Expressing a desire to study law, Wright asked the professor if it was permissible to work with licensed attorney Craven Hester, study law, and still remain a student.

> Why certainly, we have no law against that; such a case was never imagined as probable or possible. Do, however, not neglect your regular college studies, and then it is nobody's business what else you may study or learn. Our young man, sure enough, went to work at the law, Hoosier fashion...and did actually defend and win a cause...and against and from redoubtable lawyer Hester himself and with the contingent fee, he paid our treasurer the tuition price of the next term!

The industrious student who was allowed to pursue his extra-curricular goal became an Indiana governor, United States Senator, Minister to Prussia, and outlived his professor by only four years. By strange coincidence, although in separate cemeteries, the remains of Joseph Albert Wright and Baynard Rush Hall are interred in Brooklyn, New York.

Isaac Reed had begun teaching in Bloomington in 1830; likely he joined the work of Elinor's sister

Martha Young. In 1831 he was teaching the girls school Tuesdays through Fridays and continuing his missionary work in neighboring Greene County. Reed's attempts at establishing schools always seemed short-lived, likely because of the lack of enrollments. Folks on the frontiers were hard up for cash and education for their girls was not that often a priority. Also Reed was prone to moving to a new mission field or suffering from one of his intermittent illnesses. With three children to care for, Mary Ann Hall had given up teaching except perhaps for some piano students. John M. Young and Aletha became parents of a son, Wallace H. Young, in February. In May, the Halls sold a portion of their land to Vance Jones for a hundred dollars. Elinor and Isaac had a second son, Chalmers, on June 22, given the surname of a leading Scot theologian, Thomas Chalmers. That year Alexis de Tocqueville ended his monumental tour of America and had material for a monumental book. Published for the first time was the Indiana College catalog containing the names of 60 students.

Then near the end of the school year, Hall picked up his pocket *Virgil*, "left as usual on the mantel of his recitation room," and found tucked in the book an anonymous letter. The handwriting being apparently Wylie's he didn't look for a signature, but found the letter condemning him and requesting him to leave. "His (Wylie's) was the handwriting, the style, the very expressions." Baynard was certain the letter was written on Wylie's paper and that its wax seal was imprinted by Wylie's desk key. Harney agreed that the letter had all the Wylie earmarks, and even Mary Ann, bursting into tears when her husband handed her the letter without comment, exclaimed, "Oh, the Doctor must have written this!" When confronted, Dr. Wylie denied authorship, and after keeping the letter for three days purporting in order to be able to determine the writer, handed it back minus the seal. And according to Hall at one point saying, "I do candidly advise, all things considered, that you had better resign."

On September 29, stating it was because of a salary issue, Hall resigned but then agreed to stay on another year. Using salary as a reason may have been a means of avoiding further turmoil at the time, and saving face, but it also levered his annual income up to $750.00 It was no more than fair; his duties had been extended, his family was increasing, and he had to find another position, a position that made relocation a necessity.

A generation ahead, 1882, December 17, Andrew Wylie, Jr. wrote to David Banta at Bloomington:

> …the anonymous letter…was written by me without the knowledge, suggestion, remotest hint, or suspicion on the part of my Father. I was at that time a boy of sixteen years. The anonymous letter to Mr. Hall contained no more than the almost universal opinions of the students. He was indolent, careless, superficial and shamefully neglectful of his duties.

Wylie Jr. accused Hall and Harney of jealousy and made the strange statement that the two professors would hear no explanation and refused consent that an investigation should be made by the faculty. "Father became indignant and thenceforth treated them as personal enemies and wilful [*sic*] slanderers. Father offered to have every student examined, on honor, and pledged himself that whoever should be found to have written the letter he should be expelled."

Neither rescinding nor apologizing for his actions, Wylie continued,

It was an ill considered thing on my part to write such a letter, but every word of it was true, and I had no idea that it was to create so much trouble. After the trouble was created I felt impelled to come out, and avow its authorship, but was restrained...by the consideration that such avowal would be used by H. & H. as proof that their charge was substantially true, and that the letter if not written by the hand of Dr. Wylie, was written by his son at his dictation; and I retained the secret for years afterwards, even from my Father. I do not now pretend to claim that my conduct...was either wise or brave. A man of mature mind and experience would have adopted the other course. I do not know whether or not my Father ever prepared such a written account of the matter as that you refer to; I never saw, or heard of it, if he did. I have always regarded, and do now look upon the affair as beneath the serious consideration of sensible people, except for the slanders to which it gave rise and the annoyance it gave to my Father, whose nature revolted at the suggestion of a meanness and was ever at warfare with all sorts of pretenders and rascals.

Baynard Rush Hall evidently never forgave Dr. Wylie in Wylie's lifetime—Wylie, the man whom Hall called "Dr. Bloduplex," the man who with the same breath blew hot and cold. Dr. David Banta in a Foundation Day Address in January 1892 said, "Eleven years after he left Indiana College a defeated and humiliated man, he (Hall) wrote of the cause of his defeat and humiliation with a pen dipped in gall." Banta never mentioned the 1855 revision, but if Hall felt the new edition of *The New Purchase* would clean the slate, it is the earlier book that brought him recognition and praise, perhaps at the cost of redemption as well as honor for being the first to open the door of what became a huge and highly respected institution of learning and research.

Banta recorded for posterity that the author of the anonymous letter was "a Pennsylvania student."

Chapter 18

*....how our faculty spent
vacations in the woods.*

In dry times, our literati strolled into
the forests where mineralogy, botany
and natural history, (was) suggested by
dark masses of rough rocks, or curious
stones and shells, never before handled
by moderns; or by enormous wild
flowers with cups large enough to hold
two thimbles-full of dew; or by a startled
snake...or by crackling brush and whirling
leaves where shone a streak of bounding
wolf or glancing deer—(these) became
recreations detaining our friends till
dinner was deferred until tea, and tea
until supper, when all were devoured as
one!

Perhaps the mind never so marched
towards the west as once when (Hall
and Harney) and several visiting literati
were...all in a line, knee-deep and
wading...through fresh-fallen leaves and
thus discussing at one time the Greek
Tragedians, at another the Calculus and
the Analytical Geometry. Often too,
would I seduce the faculty into a hunt.
But this vacation I proposed a party to
visit and explore a cave just discovered
by a hunter in pursuit of a fox that darted
down a sinkhole and disappeared among
some rocks.

In any village, Baynard said, it's difficult to keep
a secret.

In a hilarious account of 30 adults and
unnumbered children ("who are never counted
out there, but go...as mere accretions"), Hall's
excursion to the cave and the ensuing events show
the community spirit and mutual affection of the
professor and his friends and neighbors. "Oh, it
was a glorious hubbub," when early that morning
a dozen horses were tied at the Hall hitching rack
and that many in other places.

Perhaps the increased company
was also owing to this: several affianced
lovers were of the party and rumor, with
more of romance than reality, had said
that more than two couples were to be
married in the cave under ground. Oh,

what a temptation—a Hoosier wedding
in a new-found cave. But the sternness of
truth forbids; yet the Talemaquers must
not steal this idea; when I write fiction I
shall make a story of it myself.

Vacation times being two months out of the
school year (two five-month terms for instruction),
it fell that there were spring and autumn breaks.
Hall preached on one vacation, he wrote, walking
five miles in rain to preach an hour and a half in the
open air, then walking back the same distance to
John Young's new cabin on the river.

Hall's love of hunting, his choice of the rifle over
the shotgun and his expounding the popularity of
shooting matches have precipitated the inclusion of
his work in articles written by proponents of gun
laws and anti-gun laws. When flocks of passenger
pigeons darkened the skies one autumn,

> ...with a friend I stood in an open
> space in the woods, two miles east
> of Bloomington, five hours during
> which with scarcely thirty seconds
> intermission, a stream of pigeons, about
> two hundred yards wide and average
> two layers, flowed above us...an endless
> hurricane on wings...with such an uproar
> as seemed to be prostrating the forests;
> and the deep reverberating thunder in
> the distant wilds seemed to announce
> the fall of their ponderous and ancient
> trees.

Noting that rifles were useless at bringing down single birds, horse pistols and shotguns were "sought and fixed," some with the help of Baynard's beloved friend, the village smith Austin Seward who put old pistol and gun barrels on rude stocks "to be fired in partnership—one holding the matchlock and the other 'touching her off' with an ignited stick or cigar." This necessitated improvising of powder and shot.

The upshot of one grand shoot was the separation of the hunters with their shotguns, rifles and jerry-rigged arms, and the bursting of the silver-inlaid stock of Hall's gun made for him by Seward.

"Where's Peter Batterton?" Hall asked James Borland on meeting up.

"foller'd arter the d____ pijjins."

("Don't swear, the preacher's here.")

"Did you get any?"

"Get any! Nobody didn't git none…if this ain't a jujmint on the settlemint for firing shot guns and shot out of rifles!"

The percussion had so frightened the pigeons that the grand body of the flock was never overtaken. At nearly midnight the hunters sat down at the Hall home to "an overdone, burnt up, tasteless supper— our poetry and romance all flown away with the pigeons." Batterton arrived at eight the next morning with 22 pigeons after 25 miles of walking, nursing a hand injured by the recoil or bursting of his horse pistol. The hunters, the neighbors, the church folks, the young people, those with whom the Halls had engendered relationships were thanked by him when the day came that the ties that bound them were severed; he blessed them for "past kindness and more especially for the healing of their balm-like sympathy." Austin Seward, the cherished friend and master of several crafts, restored the treasured rifle and after the publication of *The New Purchase,* laughed at the stories and verified that Baynard Rush Hall wrote truth.

Chapter 19

...a mind taught by many sorrows...

On February 14, 1832, Mary Ann Hall was brought to bed with another son, Holmes Baynard Hall, whose first name honored her mother's family and pleased Uncle John who by that time had moved to Hanover where he would be among old Presbyterian friends including Williamson Dunn. Uncle John died in that college town at age 80. Baynard with wife and growing family to support was hanging on to finish out the final year as he had agreed. Daughter Elizabeth, by now an accomplished reader, home-schooled and learned in phonics as well as sight-reading, had three little brothers to balance the preponderance of girl cousins in the Reed household. The children of the Young sisters were born into advantage, taught on a personal level in their childhoods and exposed to more than reading, writing, and "ciphering."

The 1831–32 college year saw an enrollment of 53 students; young men who divided into groups not designed for debates and declensions, but those who favored faculty and those partial to the president. Hostility between Harney and Wylie escalated during the spring exhibition of 1832 when Wylie forgot to place a student who wished to speak at the end or beginning of the program on the subject of temperance. Being put in the middle, the irate student failed to appear. At the following Saturday morning chapel, the student and Wylie locked horns and Wylie expelled the young man. The two-man faculty felt that disciplinary action should not be taken by one member of the staff without the agreement of the others.

What followed was a blistering speech by Wylie aimed at Harney and Hall in the presence of students and anyone else at chapel. Harney, a taciturn man, was sitting with one leg across the other and as all witnesses agreed, had in his hand a penknife or pocketknife (what quill-using person was without one), and was stropping it on his boot, or clicking it open and shut. Whatever the activity, it was, Hall said, a habit he had even seen Harney do in church. According to Hall's recollection, part of Dr. Wylie's response to this was, "Does he mean to stab me in the back while I explain to you his late conduct with me?"

The usually quiet Harney jumped to his feet, but Baynard grabbed his coattail and pulled him back into his chair. When Wylie finished his speech, Hall rose to give him as good as he got. The fiasco ended with Wylie announcing the dismissal of college and charging his friends to follow him out. Hall, in revealing terms, referred to this as the "celebrated Saturday," a day whose theatrics surely made the rounds of town and environs, resulting in further divisiveness. For all the squabbles the local lore adopted the sobriquet, "The Faculty Wars," and reports from the time maintain that the community split into factions. Such drama is the glue that holds factions together.

Newspapers meanwhile were recording the spread of cholera in pandemic proportions, but it was not cholera that invaded the Hall family. On Saturday, June 2, Elizabeth, born in Owen County in a log cabin eight years before, died of scarlet fever or perhaps its aftermath, pneumonia. Somehow her younger brothers and cousins survived or escaped the contagious disease. Wrote Hall,

> ...this disease appeared first and without cause in the family of Dr. Maxwell...in a few weeks, it spread carrying death and mourning into most of our habitations. It followed no known law, sometimes yielding and then refusing to yield to the same treatment, and in the same as well as different families; and often in other places resisting the established or different, or even opposite treatment...and after days and nights of ceaseless and anxious watchings, and

after fitful alternations of hope and
fear, we saw those eyes, so soft and
yet so brilliant, suddenly and strangely
quenched—as though life had retreated
thither to a last refuge and death, having
before long triumphed o'er thy dear,
dear form, did there as a last act, put out
that most precious light.

With the stoicism of that era, his faith, and the
familiarity of early and unexpected death, her Uncle
Isaac addressed those at Elizabeth's burial:

The divine hand is to be seen and
acknowledged in this death. It is a wise,
holy and mournful providence which has
opened the grave and given this tender
victim. And although we cannot now
see *why* it should be so, we believed
to the deceased child, it is well. And
to the survivors, it shall be well. Not
joyous *now*, but grievous, but its fruits
shall be righteousness to them who
are exercised therewith...Parental and
Sunday school teaching were the sources
of her knowledge. This has been a child
of prayer and religious instruction. The
good seed had taken root in her heart...

On the Sunday of Elizabeth's burial, the nine-
year-old mute son of a family whose four children
were all hearing and speech-deprived, was also
buried, the little boy having the Sunday before
stood at the coffin of a brother. Hall said he had

then spoken words of consolation over that family's coffins, and to himself, too. When he penned that chapter for the 1843 book, he stated, "I now write many things in playfulness—none in malice—yet years of my life passed when sadness only was in my heart and words and thoughts of pleasantness were impossible."

Elizabeth's grave cannot be found.

He...resigned and for weeks past had been preparing to leave the Purchase!

The trustees met in July and ended their deliberations with the recommendation that all parties involved in the college quarrel make every effort to establish peaceful working conditions. It may have been during these meetings of the board that Hall accused Wylie of ridiculing him for being a "charity" scholar at Princeton Theological, and repeating confidences and private conversations between the two. But for a time the cast of this melodrama submerged hard feelings while the Bloomington folks continued their feud between the Wylie faction and the Hall and Harney sympathizers. Hall, preparing to leave, blamed students for girdling ornamental trees he had set out years before, cutting down woodbines that shaded his doors and windows and turning pigs into his kitchen garden.

Then on a summer Sunday morning, Wylie and Harney met like Robin Hood and Little John's contentious counterparts on a narrow log walkway across a muddy section; the hewed logs ran from the college to the center of town. Baynard terms it "our sidewalk for a mile paved with wood." Each man saw the other approaching and measured his steps so they both put foot first on either end of the log and the confrontation happened in the middle. Later admitting it was deliberate and with malice aforethought, Dr. Wylie shoved Harney off the walk with one heave of a shoulder. Harney, whom Hall described as "a fine square built muscular young Kentuckian, from early life used to every feat of strength and agility," fell into the muck. He could lift a barrel of flour and carry it 50 yards without pausing, and yet, not having adopted the hair-trigger reaction, he did not retaliate. Things were no better by commencement the last week of September.

If Hall was casting his net for a position elsewhere, he does not say so. In wrapping things up, he, Mary Ann, and Aunt Doughty sold to John Harney the remainder of lot 38 in Bloomington on September 28 for $800.00. Harney may have bought this property as a quick investment. Hall sold his collection of books. What other steps he took to pack up his family and find a new place to settle is left untold. He withdrew from the college about the second week of September and did not attend the commencement ceremonies. The trustees again had tried for peace and harmony, but it was not to be. Andrew Wylie and John H. Harney had irreconcilable differences but neither was about to resign. The board faced replacing a president and an instructor. When figuratively a push came to a shove, it was again Harney who lost footing. He was dismissed by the trustees for the good of the institution; after all, instructors were more plentiful than presidents—notwithstanding that a mere young and green instructor had kept the institution going when it was teetering on its baby legs.

Isaac Reed remembered the year of Harney and Hall's exodus from the college as the year there was a famine of seed corn; that people went 50 to 150 miles to get it and "planted three and four times as much as usual in a hill."

Harney then moved his young family to Hanover where he joined the college staff and began work on what became the first American-produced algebra textbook. In his lifetime he was a college president, a newspaper publisher, and legislator. (His son, William Wallace Harney, born in Bloomington, was also an educator and popular author. John Harney's grandson Benjamin, in the early 1900s, extended the Harney name into the music world with his innovations in ragtime and blues.)

Hall said of Harney, "in an excusable moment of bitter indignation he left that, upon the whole, Best of Religious Denominations!" And that under other circumstances, the immense majority of the denomination would have "done him justice on his cruel and unrelenting foe." He wrote in the 1840s that were Harney still living, let him "know that there is one bold enough to raise a voice against the... Injustice of the Past!" John Hopkins Harney could have read *The New Purchase* in both editions. It is not known if he and Hall at later times corresponded or if he commented on what his former colleague wrote about their shared seminary history.

Andrew Wylie (a gift from heaven, said David Banta's father) steered the college into university status and for 22 years was devoted to and distinguished in the cause of higher education. As often happens, the highest praise of his character, abilities and achievements came after his death in 1851.

Ending *The New Purchase* its author wrote, about the middle of October, "a small Christian chapel was one night filled to overflowing" and those present heard a farewell address,

> ...While the voice of the wind moaning in the dying woods around came upon our hearing in fitful gusts like...passionate lamentation for the fading away of their glories. For some years this has been my home...I had once cherished the hope it was to be my home for years to come...I have shared our prosperity and adversity and in your hopes and fears, your joys and grief. We have interchanged visits of mutual good will; we have worshiped in the same temples; we have solaced each other in afflictions! We have met at the same house of feasting—alas, oftener at the same house of mourning. Yes! My children lie together in their little graves

amidst the graves of your children...
dust of mine is mingling with yours. Can
these and other ties be so unexpectedly
sundered without pain?

It was raining on the morning when the horses
and wagon were waiting. "All had been arranged
and prepared and all farewells, as we thought had
been spoke; and why should rain delay those that
had endured so many storms?" Three little boys,
their mother, and aunt Martha Young were aboard
the family's only conveyance. A sobbing Aunt
Martha Doughty had to remain with the Reeds
because, Baynard wrote, they did not know where
they were going and she must stay until they found
a resting place. Packed among meager belongings
were violin, bow and flute; the Seward rifle made
like new again was a parting gift. The pianoforte
was left behind; books left behind in the hands of
new owners, and the deepest wound, leaving two
small graves; but, wrote the father, "Alas, we had
them elsewhere too."

He had gone around the day before to say his
good-byes, but two old friends he had missed. Before
the wagon pulled away, came the intrepid hunters,
Batterton and Borland, who brought venison for
the travelers and promised them their homes would
always be open. In turn, with the typical far west
invitation of an always-unlatched door, Baynard
replied, "You will never find the string pulled in!"
whether the Halls were in log cabin or house of
brick.

Chapter 20

...there are no accidents...

In years to come, Hall would write that he had spent nearly eight years of his life in what he would always call "the purchase," an affectionate reference to a time and place where he had had great dreams, amazing adventures, "bran new" experiences, and a life the like of which he would never know again. Embarking in their wagon, with three sons from four years to eight months old and cold weather approaching, he, Mary Ann and her sister Martha left The Purchase and headed toward Philadelphia. There among old connections and familiar settings were possibilities for teachers. If this return was by the route the Halls came to Indiana, he does not say. If it was instead entirely an overland journey, it was never a subject of Hall's written memories. How long, where they stopped, how they managed the trip, he didn't record. Traveling east by a different route than when he came to Indiana may have been less expensive, but the condition of roads, traces and trails was not improved to any extent. They could have traveled a part of Zane's Trace in Ohio and passed many wagons using the finished part of the new National Road (the darling of Henry Clay), and aiming for the far west, but the exact route the Halls took will never be known. As they neared Bedford, Pennsylvania, they were entering a community settled early on by Irish, Germans and many Scots-Irish whose descendants constituted several Presbyterian churches.

Stopping at a wayside inn, tired, cold and probably hungry, the Hall children restless and fidgety, Baynard found his old wagon in need of fixing, as his cohorts in The Purchase might say. A long journey over ridges and primitive roads (and no roads) was damaging to any kind of wagon. According to a later pastor, Dr. Robert F. Sample of the Bedford Presbyterian Church, the family was "riding in a cumbrous dilapidated carriage, the driver wearing a faded camlet cloak carelessly thrown over his tall and manly frame, and a sealskin cap which partially concealed a remarkable intellectual countenance." Under the hat, his hair was nearly white although he was "not yet old." At this juncture of the trip, Philadelphia was over 200 miles away. Among the others at a busy turnpike tavern, the subject of conversation could have been the reelection of Andrew Jackson and defeat of Henry Clay, and only to a few would the entrance of strangers be of any interest.

Either another act of divine providence or a fortunate chance meeting with two former pastors of the Bedford church on Saturday brought the Reverend Baynard R. Hall into the church on Sunday morning. Having been without a steady minister for a time, the congregation was introduced that morning to a surprise minister filling in for the former pastor who had been scheduled to preach. He was the "weary, careworn and sad stranger" who had arrived the day before, and "who had been passing through the fires of affliction and dwelling much as he journeyed on the theme of 'Heaven' and continued the theme" in that service. In a few minutes the congregation concluded they were listening to no ordinary preacher, so said Dr. Sample. The following Monday, the congregation extended an invitation to Rev. Hall to lead their flock.

Sometime in the winter, Pennsylvanians would have heard of the death of Charles Carroll of Carrolton, the last of the Signers of the Declaration of Independence; the venerable Marylander died that November at the age of 95.

In the spring, 1833, the Carlisle, Pennsylvania Presbytery received Baynard's request to be installed at Bedford and relieved of his membership in the Vincennes, Indiana Presbytery. In the meantime he was permitted to administer ordinances and perform the duties of pastor in the Bedford church. In the fall, for some reason not recorded, the call from the church made no commitment as to salary and thinking of establishing a school, Hall, on his part, agreed to be the stated supply pastor and would remain so until leaving in 1838. Records do not show exactly when Hall began the Bedford Classical and Mathematical Academy, but it was his second foray into the business of operating a private boarding school, having overseen Mary Ann and Martha's Bloomington school. He came to the community with two veteran teachers on board.

In Bedford, Pastor Hall baptized two children on their death beds, one an infant nine months of age, in late summer. Before the first anniversary of their arrival there, Baynard and Mary Ann buried Baynard Chisholm, almost three and a half years old, in the Presbyterian cemetery. He, and maybe the others, did not survive whooping cough, another of the dreaded childhood diseases. In Hanover, John Morris Young, Jr. was born.

In 1834 after having begun another church in Jackson County, Indiana, Isaac with Elinor Reed advertised a school for males and females to open in Bloomington in a new house Reed built. He started a church in Spencer, Owen County and supplied half the time, while teaching at home through the week. Then after another round of moving about, the Reeds settled in Hanover. In a letter from Hanover where she was staying with nephew John M. Young in 1835, Aunt Doughty wrote to Mary Ann and Martha in Bedford, a typical family letter: Baby John Morris Jr. had gotten over weaning; she thanked them for a box of presents and wished she could see the hands that packed them up.

I have paid one visit to Bloomington since you left us, with the exception of one last August. I went over in February and returned in April, and visited all our old friends...Mrs. Parks at your old House, Mrs. Eliot at Mr. Harney's old house and Mrs. Perren at Mrs. Wallace's old house. I went no where but to the places where I was sent for, and there was a large party at every house, but never saw one of the W's (underlined) at any of them, tho I heard her extolled very highly as an excellent cook and housekeeper. I have had my last visits in Bloomington, I think—I attended a three days meeting in the Steel settlement, the third sabbath in July; it was the first sacrament I have attended since you left us—they have moved the meetinghouse into the Steel settlement there near the old school house.

She wrote that "a great many had inquired after Mr. Hall and you (you, underlined) and said they would like to hear him preach again."

Aunt Doughty ended her letter to the family at Bedford saying, "I have a thousand things to tell you if I could see you."

We prefer an admixture of various and opposite studies.

"It was appointed by a charter," wrote Professor

Hall, when he was one-half the faculty at the Bloomington college, "that the faculty should oversee the Students; the Trustees oversee the Faculty; the Board of Visitors, the Trustees; and the Legislature the Visitors; the people in general engaging to oversee the Legislature, the people of Bloomington, the entire whole! The cause of education was, then, well *overseen!*" With an unhappy experience behind him when he arrived in Bedford, but well endowed with ideas and equipped with theories, here he found an opportunity to establish a school of his own. The Bedford Academy was operating as early as 1833, beginning on a small scale, but according to local history, within a year it had "upwards" of a hundred young people who came from Pennsylvania, New Jersey, Maryland, Virginia, Ohio, Louisiana and even Canada.

The town of Bedford had a rich military history; Baynard Hall would have known of the British fort there about two decades before the Revolution. The community in an Allegheny valley had been Washington's headquarters during the Whiskey Rebellion when the commander-in-chief, Alexander Hamilton, and Henry "Light Horse Harry" Lee, brought almost 13,000 militia into western Pennsylvania to quell a tax revolt.

Whether the academy was called The Bedford Classical and Military Academy as one historian put it, or The Bedford Classical and Mathematical Academy as Hall named it in 1835, the school had its military drills at least for a time. Hall's brochure printed in July 1835 stated, under

> Arms: A requisition having been lately made on the General Government by the Adjutant general of this Commonwealth,—*one hundred Cadet Musquets, with the accoutrements,* are included for the *use of the Bedford Classical and Mathematical Academy.* These guns, like the heavy musquets already used by the pupils will, in lieu of flints, have pieces of wood; and never be used except in the presence and under the direction of the Preceptors. About *forty minutes* every morning at day break, and about *one hour* every Saturday afternoon, is the only time spent in the Drills and Parades; which, after the experience of nearly a year, are found to answer all the important uses originally designed in making military exercises a small part of the Academical instruction and discipline.

Willliam Schell wrote, "the boys were required to wear a uniform and parade at 6 a.m. and carried wooden muskets of the regulation size and color, with bored barrel, ramrod, imitation iron locks, bands, etc. They were made to resemble the army muskets in every particular." Stating the quality of material is unimportant, Hall's brochure outlined the required color blue for fall and winter uniforms and dark blue summer cloth for summer and announced that residing in Bedford were excellent workmen who could make uniforms.

Studies included the usual penmanship, and geography, arithmetic, grammar, Belles Lettres, history, logic, mental and moral philosophy, "mathematics and natural philosophy—as extensively as in ordinary College Courses," original compositions, orations, Bible recitations, Latin, Greek, Hebrew, French, Italian, Spanish and German, Scott's Military Exercises and instrumental music, with the study of music and modern languages optional. Books were available to buy at the Academical Book Store. April and August were vacation months with a short intermission from Christmas until New Year's.

The first session fee was $8.50 with every subsequent session, $7.50. Taxes for summer session were 25 cents and for fall and winter, 75 cents. The largest expense listed was $10.00 for one or two musical instruments per quarter at three lessons per week; and $10.00 for piano lessons per quarter at five lessons a week. Fines were imposed on students for certain "inadvertencies, errors and offences."

"Female students (exempted of course from all inconsistent studies and duties) although on some occasions and in some mental exercises purposely and advantageously associated with the other pupils, are for the most part, separately instructed, counseled, and admonished." Students living within the school facilities paid for their boarding, lodging, wood and candles $2.00 per week with "washing included at two dollars, fifty-seven and a half cents per week." Boarding was also allowed with respectable families in Bedford.

Among the girls enrolled at Bedford was Martha Doughty Reed, then 15, and the oldest of Isaac and Elinor's children. In their most recent move, Martha had left her friends, the Lowe and Howe girls, and what had been for a time a stable home in Bloomington. (In the summer of 1837, Martha wrote, "I was truly rejoiced to learn Elizabeth Howe is married, but I hope Louisa will remain single until I return; for it would afford me great pleasure to see and call her Miss Howe again.")

The 1835 faculty included a familiar name, that of Selby Harney, a younger brother of John Hopkins Harney. Selby taught with a bachelor's degree. Martha Morris Young was the only woman faculty member. The remainder of the staff were William G. Allen, A.B., Lieutenant John G. Martin, James King, and John S. Compher.

An enterprising promoter, Baynard Hall called upon influential people to aid his cause and among those as his references were Professor George Bush, his old friend and former clerical colleague who was on staff at what became New York University (Bush published the first American definitive study of Islam and a grammar of the Hebrew language), Hall's former mentor Rev. William Latta, Congressman Jacob Mann, William J. Duane, a former Secretary of the Treasury; Alexander Thompson, a judge and congressman; James Reeside, one of the largest mail contractors in the United States; Elderkin Potter, a prosecuting attorney; Harm Jan Huidekoper, a Unitarian philanthropist; and about all the lawyers of the Bedford bar, among others.

Baynard probably journaled his time at Bedford, but nothing remains; he did complete an original work in 1835. Leaving Selby Harney in charge of the school, he spent the winter of 1835 in Philadelphia overseeing the publication of his Latin grammar, a 140-page book titled *Exercises, Analytical and Synthetical; Arranged for the New and Compendious Latin Grammar.* The title page lists the author: "By Baynard R. Hall, A.M., Principal of the Bedford Classical and Mathematical Academy, and formerly Professor of the Ancient Languages in the College of Indiana." Harrison Hall, not a relative, printed the book in 1836, and was also its major seller. While in the city Baynard became ill and wrote to Mary Ann in Bedford to come; she complied with his wish and took their son Rush with her. Niece Martha at the school surmised that the illness was homesickness. That visit may have led to another production, the birth in 1836 of a daughter, Edistina Morris Hall. A downturn in the economy of the United States marked the year 1837. Near the end of the year 29-year-old Selby Harney died. He was buried beside toddler Baynard Chisholm Hall in the Presbyterian cemetery. Neither grave is marked by a headstone.

Chapter 21

*A school is sometimes called
the world in miniature.*

In 1835, the Isaac Reed family left Bloomington, making their next home in Hanover where they reunited with John M. Young, Uncle John, friend Williamson Dunn, and other Presbyterian associates. Through 1836, Isaac traveled in Kentucky and Ohio and arrived at home to find his son Chalmers recovering from a nearly fatal illness. The Reed family then spent time in Shelby County, Indiana, where they had a short-term school and Elinor and the children attended courses on elocution. Elinor obtained a teaching certificate in that subject. They went again to Kentucky, back to Hanover, and ended up in Putnamville, Indiana, with another school that did not last. They went to Paris, Illinois, and then by the beginning of 1838, they were back in Indiana, residing in Terre Haute. Daughter Martha was left at Hanover in 1835 with her Uncle John and Aunt

Aletha Young until in the fall when John escorted her to the Bedford Academy. Writing to her parents in October, 15-year-old Martha reviewed her arrival at the new school in Pennsylvania.

Dear Mama,

...The next morning after we left Hanover... we arrived at Cincinnati. There we changed boats, and stayed until 12 o'clock, at which hour we left for Pittsburgh; and we got there on the following Sabbath, where we remained until the next day. We then took the stage for Bedford, and reached here Tuesday at three o'clock. We were just 24 hours traveling one hundred and fifty miles. When we got to uncle Hall's house, the first room we got into was Mr. Allen's; the first person I saw was aunt Mary at the top of a pair of winding stairs; uncle Hall met us in the entry and put one arm around uncle Young's neck and the other around mine. We did not see aunt Martha until we reached the study room. They live in a three story house; there are two small school rooms and one large one, where we assemble every morning for prayer, at six o'clock. Besides these there is a sitting room, kitchen and hall in the first story. In the second story there are the front and the back parlors. Aunt Mary's room, uncle Hall's study, a spare bedroom and a most splendid entry—the ceiling is carved splendidly. In the third story there are six rooms; one of them is aunt Martha's and mine.

There are four gentlemen teachers besides uncle Hall. Mr. Allen is professor of modern languages; Mr.

Harney is professor of mathematics; Mr. Cumpher and Mr. King have the primary department. Uncle Hall superintends the whole. I am studying Latin, French and Music and reviewing all my former studies.

Mr. Allen says in two years I will make a splendid French scholar. Aunt says I will play elegantly...I shall learn to paint; they teach it in the school and in the most elegant manner possible. There is the plainest set of people here which you ever saw; they wear a calico dress in church, with capes of the same, and have bonnets of the same shape as Mrs. Smith's in Bloomington, lined with green silk and trimmed with the same colored ribbon but entirely plain. The girls wear calico and worsted dresses to school and church. Aunt Martha and I sit up every night until between nine and ten o'clock, studying. I have not been sick a minute since I started from Indiana; my cheeks are the very picture of health. I had a little cold after I got here, but no cough.

In her next letter she writes that most scholars are from a distance. That she hadn't known what constant study was until she came to Bedford and,

> ...if you miss three lessons in succession, you are suspended until you bring a written cause from parent or guardian; if you have no excuse you are fined a half dollar...I am entirely at home; aunt and uncle are as kind to me as they possibly can be. I have enjoyed excellent health ever since I have been here.

Indeed you would hardly know me—
my cheeks are so red.

Later writing as she began her 16th year, Martha expected it to be her last at school. She missed her younger sisters and brothers, as well as her parents. Speaking of her brothers, she related, "There are a good many little boys here who are as young as Whitefield and they all wrote their compositions and spoke them at the exhibition before the assembly of five hundred persons." She wrote to her father at Christmas, "This day when you all sit together, though there be one absent, still she is with you in mind, and when you bend the pious knee I know your Martha is not forgotten." She wrote that Uncle Hall had married a couple and the wedding party rode 10 miles to a dinner; the sleigh he was in upset in a bank of snow while coming home. When her family moved to Putnam County, she told her parents, "Indiana will be a great state before many years. Uncle Hall said Papa should have kept his land in New Albany for he could have got as many thousands for it now as hundreds then. I am becoming very attached to Uncle Hall because he always speaks in such a very affectionate manner of you all..."

As the 1837 depression continued to grip the country, and attendance at the school was falling off, Martha quoted her uncle as saying it would not take much to make him resign professional life and go into farming. Baynard published in *The Bedford Gazette* in September an interview with Captain

John Holliday, a survivor of the Goliad massacre of Texan prisoners of war in Mexico in 1836. Holliday was visiting relatives in Bedford.

In a letter to attorney Samuel Barclay the next spring, Hall reported his students were down to 30 from 60 and that he and Martha M. Young were the sole teachers. The competition of common schools was becoming a threat. He stated,

> I can do without a charter, but if it will subvene the interests of my townsmen, I am content under certain conditions that my school may become the 'incorporated' one. I must remain in it as long as I wish and no interference must be used with my price, plans &c—other than to entitle us to the appropriations.

Hall considered going to Hanover. With his Presbyterian network still intact, he may have been able to secure a position there, but niece Martha indicated in a letter that her Uncle Hall did not want to go to Hanover and neither did she. For him, it would be a step back into a staff position; for her, continued separation from her parents.

She wrote her mother the next month, "Uncle Hall is sitting just behind me, playing the violin." Martha had then spent three happy years with Baynard and Mary Ann Hall, but she was eager to return to her own family. She wrote in the fall of 1837, "When I get home, M'a, I want to take the care of the house off of you. I am not half ready to get married. If I only get home once more I shall be satisfied."

In the cycle of birth and death, on March 25, 1838, Carolina Baynard Hall was born in Bedford. Baynard wrote a discourse, "Disciplined Youth Necessary for the Duties and Comfort of Old Age." Then the Halls left Bedford for Bordentown, New Jersey.

Martha Doughty Reed died April 8, 1839 at age 18, at yet another temporary residence of her parents, and was buried at Terre Haute. "I experienced one of the most afflictive events of my life in which trials & afflictions had been so frequent & prevalent," wrote Isaac Reed. "This death almost broke her mother's heart & to me it weakened much of my attachment to life...Our first born child; our grown up, educated, accomplished daughter Martha."

...teaching is a holy vocation.

The teacher, as an artist, possesses intellectual and moral qualifications that must class him with the best, and show that his office or profession ranks among the highest in dignity and importance. The teacher must be, among other things, a philosopher, a judge, a ruler, a parent, a preacher; and he must be also learned and scientific. He must have power over himself. He must be conversant with men as well as books. He must be disinterested. He must possess an ardent love of learning, and must delight in his creations...And this spirit, and this enthusiasm, make him press onward through difficulties and discouragements, and over obstacles and impediments...pupils must be regarded as his children...times are when he must preach to them... he must warn, rebuke, entreat; he must pray with them in public, and for them in private; he must love them; he must rejoice with their joy, and mourn with their grief.

Martha Doughty Reed's death in the spring of 1839 followed the relocation of the Halls to New Jersey. Losing that beloved niece who had been so much a surrogate daughter was another wrenching blow. At this time a review of Hall's Latin grammar published in *The Literary and Theological Review* was unduly unkind to the author. Hall's stint in Bordentown creates a gap in his story; the few items in an otherwise missing paper trail are his officiating at a wedding in 1839, and brief mentions that he taught and preached in Bordentown and Trenton, and served as principal of academies in both. In late August 1839, he delivered an address to the young women of Spring-Villa Seminary in Bordentown on the occasion of an awards night.

In October 1841 while living in Trenton, he conveyed 200,320 acres of his father's 1795 land grant to a Pennsylvania corporation operating under the name of The North Carolina Land Company. Four shareholders paid a total of $75.00. The last record found in quieting the title of this land is in 1927.

On the 96th anniversary of the College of New Jersey in September 1842, Baynard Hall was again the recipient of an honorary master's degree. At

Trenton, what was happening with the Halls can't be traced with any certainty except that Baynard was installed as first stated supply pastor at the Second Presbyterian Church when it was organized in November 1842, until a regular pastor was hired in the spring of 1843. Back in Indiana, brother-in-law John M. Young and his wife, Aletha, came to a parting of their ways.

During the years since their days in Indiana, Hall was writing memories and recollections intent on a book—neither a textbook, nor a book of sermons, or a romantic novel. It became a book which he refused to categorize even as autobiographical. Unknowingly, the teacher painstakingly produced a book that would educate future generations about a unique time and place, people and events— a priceless, primary source that in another century would be called "an imperishable Indiana classic." It would also create a storm of criticism.

Another move sent the Halls from Trenton to Poughkeepsie in Dutchess County, New York, a progressive town on the Hudson River with a number of schools and churches. In Putnam County, Indiana, Lydia Ann Lapsley Reed had married a young gentleman farmer named Worthington Williams, whose father Josiah Williams of Poughkeepsie bought land in Putnam County. Worthington had come to the county about 1836. Through Hall's niece Lydia, familiarly called Ann by all the family, Hall became friends with her husband and the two men exchanged letters. Baynard wrote from

Poughkeepsie in early June 1843:

> My dear Sir, When removing hither,
> I met your father...and requested him to
> inform you that I was to be connected
> with Mr. Bartlett's Institution on College
> Hill. Since then I have had little time to
> attend to anything else than its peculiar
> duties. We live at the corner of Conklin
> and Mill street in Van Benthylin's house.
> I walk up and down four times daily.
>
> Next week will be published at New
> York 3000 Broadway by D. Appleton &
> Co & in Philadelphia Chestnut Street by
> Geo S. Appleton, 'The New Purchase, or
> Seven and a Half Years in the Far West
> by Robert Carlton Esq' in 2 vols.

Baynard Hall, the educator, found a niche in Charles Bartlett's Collegiate College. Also a graduate of Union College and a practitioner of Nott's kind and gentle treatment of students, Bartlett had opened the school in 1836, a new building resembling the Parthenon, located on College Hill just east of Poughkeepsie. From the summit of the hill could be seen the town, the Hudson, and the Catskills. Bartlett's school stressed education in a family atmosphere despite the fact it was a classical institution. Discipline was not administered by beatings, but "by rewards and punishments of an intellectual and moral nature addressed to the understanding of the heart." Students at Bartlett's were from well-to-do Hudson River families. They were taught the classic languages, French, Spanish, rhetoric, logic, natural philosophy, mathematics and history with an emphasis on American history. One of the boys who might have been at the school as a day student when Hall arrived was one of the children of an old Dutch-descent family from the Hudson Valley. He was James Roosevelt, the future father of Franklin Delano Roosevelt.

Hall, the author, may have been celebrated in New York when his new book appeared in the shops in 1843, but back in Bloomington, it caused a stir as the locals and students at Indiana University, as it was now called, flipped through pages looking for people they could recognize despite the writer's fanciful names and his own pseudonym, Robert Carlton. In ending his letter to Williams in Putnam County, Baynard requests:

> By all means procure yourself a copy—& as the author a friend of ours will receive no profit unless half the edition is sold within certain limits, he will be grateful if you can aid in selling some two or three dozen copies in your region.

> Would you guess at the true author you will see in the book reason enough for concealing his name—at least until the disclosure comes from other quarters.

He was pleased that the book "sold immediately even at $1.50, and in the midst of the Cheap

Literature Age, when English works were selling for a shilling." In that spring of 1843, the country lost one of its better known authors, Noah Webster.

Baynard and Mary Ann were training their children for their futures. Rush was 15 and a talented artist; Holmes was a 12-year-old, showing an ability to write. The girls, Edistina, seven, may have been foreshadowing health problems, but was destined to be a fine pianist, her father said. Her sister Carolina Baynard Hall was five and might have been singing nursery rhymes about c-o-w-s.

Two sons, two daughters; it was an ideal family.

The Reverend John Finley Crowe, who had opened a little grammar school in Hanover in 1827, recorded in his book of parishioners of the Hanover Presbyterian Church, the death of a good and faithful servant, John Holmes, November 1844.

Chapter 22

I have long discerned the hands of a gracious Providence.

The first edition of *The New Purchase* was printed in two volumes at the same time and in a run of a thousand. All in all, the comments and reviews were favorable. It marked a success that inspired Baynard to write another. Tongue in cheek, he claims in the preface to *Something for Every Body: Gleaned in the Old Purchase, from Fields Often Reaped,* that this book is a departure from old topics, even though he had promised a kind of sequel to his first book. It was another original Hall and in an age of flowery prose, he would again break the mold:

> ...every elevation, hill or mountain... has been ascended and from the summit every scene of lake or land described, poetized, painted! Every meadow has

been measured, every water befished; every woman, in or out of pantalettes and tournures, besonneted; every thing galvanized, phrenologized, mesmerized; in short, that every body has seen all places, is acquainted with every body else, and knows, in all matters, more than ever was known before, or ever can be known again.

Using his two alter egos, Robert Carlton and Charles Clarence, the book is a series of letters between the two personages of "incidents, narratives, and illustrative anecdotes strictly... some of them almost verbally, true..." The book is an exuberant exposition of Hall's opinions and observations on numerous subjects: theology, medicine, capital punishment (a gallows at the edge of town indicates the community provides its citizens safety), temperance, contemporary trends (unlike Brooklyn writer Walt Whitman, Hall scoffs at phrenology) and in the process he added more of his own history. Published not quite quickly enough to ride into public favor on the heels of *The New Purchase,* he labored over it during his tenures in New Jersey and Poughkeepsie. Also published by the Appletons, *Something for Every Body* was in the shops in 1846.

During that time of teaching and writing, Hall certainly followed news of the acquisition of Texas as a U.S. Territory, and possibly he read with his youngsters new adventures, *The Count of Monte*

Cristo and *The Three Musketeers.* In 1845, Rev. James W. Alexander, a Presbyterian minister, graduate of Princeton, former professor, and pastor of a New York City church, invited Hall to preach for him in a Sunday service in the fall. The two were near in age, had been pastors in Trenton, and may have known each other for many years.

The Poughkeepsie years were pleasant enough; the association with Bartlett's Collegiate School was a good thing to have on one's resume', but Charles Bartlett was master of his school and a school cannot serve two masters. Baynard never records a date or reasons, but this association came to an end and he became principal of the Dutchess Academy in Dutchess County, an institution chartered in 1792 and housed in a new building in Poughkeepsie in 1836. At Dutchess, Hall was not only the principal but taught his classical languages, elocution, composition, spelling and reading for a compensation of the income of the school and an appropriation from a Literature Fund. Each year, he was required to pay $400.00 to be applied to the debt and insurance on the building. The principal was also required to keep up repairs, and employ and pay all the teachers and himself. Hall supervised about a half a dozen teachers; the number of students is unknown, but in earlier years there had been more than 100. As in other communities, there was an increase in the number of public schools and private schools felt the pinch of decreasing enrollments.

The school admitted males and females with the senior department, as it was called, exclusively for males. A juvenile department had been added under Hall's leadership; his daughters Edistina, 10, and Carolina, two years younger, had completed recitations there in a summer term.

At the November 1846 meeting of the trustees it was reported that the committee appointed to raise funds had not succeeded in raising subscriptions to any amount. That Hall preferred not to function under trustees can be inferred by his consulting with the board in regard to leasing or buying the school. In January, the negotiations for buying the school continued, but by the end of February, Baynard had tendered his resignation to be effective at the end of the term. In the March meeting, trustees accepted his resignation, releasing him from all liability after he paid the rent up to May.

After leaving the Dutchess Academy, Hall became principal of the Newburgh Academy in another Hudson River town, halfway between New York City and Albany in a picturesque rural area. In Newburgh, Washington had his headquarters at the end of the Revolution. And in another bid for total freedom, on July 26, 1847, the "American" Liberians in Africa after decades of efforts by the American Colonization Society, declared themselves independent. This fulfilled the desires of those who wished to return to Africa, those who wished American Africans to leave the United States, and those whose efforts and desires were sincerely altruistic (although too simplistic), believing that a relocation to what was near to being a homeland was the ideal solution to the race issue. Intellectually and emotionally invested in this societal wrangle, Hall kept an eye on the progress of the ACS, and germinated the idea for a novel. In the meantime, he produced in 1848, *Teaching a Science: The Teacher as Artist,* which he introduced by writing, "This book is not an experiment, but an experience." Chapters included the science or the end of teaching, tools and instruments, arranging and managing material, schools in their kinds, sorts and varieties; common schools, and before a message to the young, he wrote a timely chapter, "Persons most suitable for Teachers."

In an extended essay, Rev. James W. Alexander, the author's friend, ventured that the worst thing about the book was its title. Nevertheless, Alexander gives a peer's view of Hall's work, praising *and* disagreeing, finding merit and voicing objections. He summed Baynard's efforts: "...far from making the business of education an easy or an irresponsible affair, he plainly regards it as a high solemnity." (Some of Hall's theories and ideas are timely and applicable for today.) In 1848, *Teaching a Science: The Teacher as Artist,* may have been the catalyst for Baynard's next recognition, an honorary Doctor of Divinity from Rutgers. Honorary degrees were not wasted on Rev. Hall.

...every reason to love his profession.

In June 1847, Hall wrote to his friend Worthington Williams in Indiana, extolling the virtues of their situation in Newburgh and sharing the news,

> ...information about our relatives here and queries about our relatives there. We are situated in the most beautiful place in the world—certainly on the Hudson. The lower Newburgh is perhaps a Natchez under the hill as to beauty—but upper Newburgh is of surpassing beauty. Our Academy is unparalleled for beauty of property. We see up and down nearly 20 miles—I can without a glass see the buildings at West Point 8 miles below. Our house is very convenient and very pretty—it will accommodate 38 boarders. It is separate from the Academy buildings in which we teach.

> We began with 36 students. Eight are boarders. We have very fair prospects and indeed reason and nature here both say we ought to succeed—if we have time to make an impression. I have just completed my Gymnasium. It will cost about $500. I paid today $395. This is a new feature in education. My sons are superb gymnasts. Rush is the teacher.

My last book was very popular. About 900 copies have been sold. I reap small profit—books are so cheap. I shall, if spared, write perhaps another work. I do not know what exactly—it begins to form up, but rather misty and indistinct.

Many very important and satisfactory reasons sent us to this place. Among others, the D.C. Academy was ruined by the free schools—and the building was so out of repair that it would have swamped us into $10,000! Here, if we buy, $5,000 will do as much as $12,000 at Poughkeepsie. And if I do not buy, I can do without important repairs. We are and were never so admirably suited in any respect.

We are all well. A. Doughty is a wonderful old lady! She is like a woman of 40—while she is more than 70!

Rush B. Hall is 19 nearly. He teaches my preparatory school—also Music, Drawing, Gymnasium. Holmes B. Hall is nearly 16—he teaches writing. John Young, son of Glenville, is with us. I shall make him a teacher. Edistina is 10. She is a fine Latin scholar of her years. She is a very fine pianist and if she lives is destined to great and wonderful excellence in Music. Carolina is 9 about.

Hall concludes by suggesting Williams send his son Josiah to Newburgh to live with his great aunts, uncle, and cousins. The reference to Edistina's destiny is an indication that another member of the Holmes-Reed-Young family circle does not have perfect health.

Chapter 23

...what an evil is the system.

By 1850, the Halls were still living in a Newburgh home with boarding students. Proud of his sons Rush, 22, and Holmes, 19, Baynard had made them teachers. But the two young men had not broken away from home. The hired help included Irish Catharine McCann, and a 16-year-old girl, Bridget, who may have been her sister, and Martha Smith, an African American. Among the extended family living there were John Morris Young in the mercantile business, his sons Wallace who worked as a carpenter, and John Jr., the nephew whom, at 13, Hall had promised to make a teacher. Martha M. Young, still a spinster, and about 14 students rounded out the household.

In 1851, Harriet Beecher Stowe's *Uncle Tom's Cabin* was appearing in serial form. As the public—those who read, and those who heard about it—began to be stirred by the novel, Hall was delivering chapters to Charles Scribner in New York, titled *Frank Freeman's Barber Shop: A Tale,* by Rev. Baynard R. Hall, D.D. Whether Hall intended to compete with Stowe's work as an inciting or insightful story, *Frank Freeman* was reviewed by contemporaries as a reply to Stowe, a great book, a worthless book, and both an illustration of slavery's evils and the benefits of bondage. The reviews reflect the seeming ambiguities in the book, a novel set with Hall's portrayals from firsthand and subjective experience of slave-owners. He goes after those abolitionists who promote rebellion and put runaways in jeopardy and a different kind of servitude, aims to show there are slave-owners who are not Simon Legrees, and aligns himself with the advocates of a free Liberia. He does not defend dealers. The work is fodder for slavery issues and as always in analyzing a Baynard Hall production, the moderns have ignored checking his background, as in the writer who mockingly notes Hall's claim to be somewhat a "southerner," but points out the author lived in Brooklyn, New York.

Hall slips an anecdotal love story into the book, draws on his roots in South Carolina, and does not let his readers forget that he is a minister of the gospel. In 1852, a writer in *The New York Evangelist* snarls, "Instances of intense toadyism to slavery are so common, that the only thing noticeable in this is its source...it will do no harm, for it essays a hopeless task." By contrast an unsigned article in *The New York Observer and Chronicle:* "There is great power in the book, and when once the reader lays hold of it, he will not wish to leave it till he has made an end of it." The book does have its own power and deserves to be noticed in any study of the subject of race in America. *Godey's Ladys Book,* Philadelphia, rightly described Hall's treatment as a "new course on the subject." Rush B. Hall sketched no incendiary drawings for *Frank Freeman.* The 23-year-old Bloomington, Indiana native, showing promise as an artist, was not there to illustrate his father's next book.

There's every possibility with Baynard's keen insight into human behavior and attitudes and the events of the times, *Frank Freeman* was born before *Uncle Tom.* The Compromise of 1850 had been passed with its controversial and conscience-rending Fugitive Slave Law. Clergy and lay people alike kept abreast of and argued the burgeoning issue of slavery in America. A product of his day and culture, Hall recorded the ugly euphemisms and ethnic slurs as honest depictions of ordinary speech, words that are rightfully shunned today.

Thirty years later in 1882, Louise Clarke Pyrnelle wrote a children's book about plantation life. In her preface she laments, "there are no more dear old mammies and aunties...." She wrote, "Nor does my little book pretend to be any defense of slavery. I know not whether it was right or wrong (there are many pros and cons on the subject)..."

And Hall: "...the slave-dealer!—that speculator in human limbs and sinews!—that wretch that looks at a man's jaw as at a horse's!" The character *Frank Freeman* prays, "May God dispose that land of the South, and show them some way to let you go free!"

Scribner published the book in 1852; it appeared again in 1853 by Alden, Wanzer, Beardsley & Co., under a more impressive cover, and in 1854 by Burnett and Bostwick, New Orleans. In the storm of attention surrounding Rev. Henry Ward Beecher's sister's sad tale of inhumanity, Hall's story of a free African American who becomes his own man in his own country isn't grabbed off the shelves. It did not greatly boost the work of the American Colonization Society, but as predicted, it did no harm. No record of the number of copies produced can be found.

Rev. Baynard R. Hall, D.D. was a keynote speaker for the literary societies at the June 1852 commencement and anniversary of Nassau Hall at Princeton. His two-hour speech, titled *Prodesse Quam Conspici,* the Cliosophian Motto, was described as "liberal and wise counsels." The motto loosely translates into the advice: Be useful or accomplished rather than conspicuous, and was borrowed from Miami University. The ceremonies were reported in *The Trenton State Gazette* alongside the news of the death of Henry Clay.

The Isaac Reeds were again separated; Isaac far afield in his missionary travels while Elinor and children lived with her married daughter Lydia Ann Williams on a Putnam County, Indiana, farm. Elinor struggled with money problems in the continual keeping of the wolf from the door, as did the Halls, who moved to Brooklyn. If Rev. Hall had been pastoring a church in Newburgh, he left no facts about that. It was in Newburgh and Poughkeepsie that he became familiar with the Dutch Reformed Church prevalent in those places and he was becoming a more liberal Presbyterian.

Hall in his preface to *Frank Freeman* wrote, "the essence of our tale is truth, while the embodying of the truth is fiction; that *nearly every* leading incident *separate* from its place in the story, is a fact and not a few of these passed under the eyes of the author; and...in several scenes, he was...an actor." Baynard Hall wrote about what he knew.

Elinor Reed writing to Isaac, who was on missions in Kentucky: "Is all still with regard to the negros? I hope so, but I do not wish to live again in the interior of a slave State."

Chapter 24

...every noble thing demands a sacrifice.

When the Halls relocated to Brooklyn, it was still within a rural farming area, but on its way to being a prosperous city and considered a part of Long Island. The family lived in a three-story frame house, one of the earliest in town, and possibly constructed by housebuilder Walter Whitman, father of the poet. Walt Whitman, quietly writing *Leaves of Grass* during the 1850s, was then a Brooklyn journalist. Rev. Henry Ward Beecher was also a fellow resident and pastor of a Congregationalist Church. Beecher and Hall were in agreement on some points of the slavery issue; Beecher opposed encouraging slaves to escape and spoke against the Compromise of 1850. That Hall and Beecher met is not beyond reason. Some astute reader of *Frank Freeman* may be able to tease out of Baynard's enigmatic prose references to Beecher, perhaps as in the person "intoxicated" by fame. The two outspoken clergymen could have compared their tenures in Indiana.

All the rooms in Hall's three-story Cumberland Street home were fitted with fireplaces—in the parlor Hall could poke the embers and remember the Owen County cabin. The lower floor was a little below street level with a cellar beneath. That lower floor was the kitchen area opening onto the backyard. Not far away was a creek that has long since been covered over. Whether this building housed his Park Institute is debatable, but that is the name under which he operated his next boarding school.

The transfer to Brooklyn from Newburgh may have been another decision based on economics. In Brooklyn, Hall managed the institute and preached at the Dutch Reformed Church. By 1860, his real estate was valued at $4,500.00. Along with preaching and teaching, Baynard was also available for lectures. Following the publication of *Frank Freeman,* he was inspired to revise and release *The New Purchase* and began negotiating for a publisher and contacting influential friends and acquaintances to promote the sale of the forthcoming edition.

Park Institute was advertised in *The Brooklyn Eagle* in 1853 as it began its fourth quarter. The display ad states the school is for both sexes who are separately instructed in separate rooms and with separate yards and entrances. "Rev. B.R. Hall, D.D. Principal and Proprietor, who has been a teacher for more than thirty years, is aided by several well-qualified instructors; and the course of studies mainly classical and mathematical, includes the elementary and higher English branches." Fees were from $8.00 to $16.00 per quarter of 11 weeks and to be paid in advance. Instrumental music from $15.00 to $20.00. Modern Languages and Drawing, each $5.00 per quarter. Boarding scholars paid $65.00 per quarter which included tuition in regular studies with the use of textbooks and stationery, and bed, bedding, light, fuel and washing.

The house on Cumberland would be the final home for not just Baynard and Mary Ann, but Aunt Doughty, Martha Young, and the remaining Hall children. The first death in that house made necessary the purchase of another piece of real estate, a large plot in the Cemetery of the Evergreens outside of town on Jamaica Bay.

Rush Baynard Hall was dying when he illustrated *Frank Freeman*. At 26, he had never left his parents. Pulmonary consumption was listed as the cause of his death—a disease common, contagious, and easy to diagnose. Night sweats, fevers, coughing, flushed cheeks, the loss of weight that spawned the term—symptoms seen in more than one member of the Hall and Reed families. The bacillus for tuberculosis could lie dormant in the body for years. Rush died on Sunday morning, March 12, 1854, at home.

The funeral notice in *The New York Times* read, "The relatives and friends of the family are respectfully requested to attend his funeral from the residence of his father, on Tuesday, March 14, at 3 o'clock P.M. Newburgh and Poughkeepsie papers please copy."

Rush's father knew the signs of tuberculosis; in *Frank Freeman* he wrote of a character having a "slight occasional cough; a very little pain in his breast; a blushing spot now and then perceptible on his cheek...."

Mrs. Henry Ward Beecher, no stranger to premature deaths, wrote, "...who can hear that fearful sound—the heavy fall of the earth on the coffin's lid—unmoved?" For the pastor and his wife, they "go back to their silent abode to resume laborious duties...to force back into the deepest recesses of their own hearts the ever-present consciousness of their loss. All this sorrow must be battled with in silence...they may not falter and sink beneath personal griefs." Like the Halls, the Beechers had also left two small graves in Indiana.

This loss of his much-loved son could have pushed Hall into the busy toil of adapting *The New Purchase* for a second edition, a labor that might have helped dispel the ever-present consciousness of loss. How did Mary Ann Hall, the mother who had heard the earth fall on the coffins of six children, deal with her sorrow? "Griefs and sorrows deeply seated rarely use words...," wrote the father.

Two months later back in Bloomington, Dr. David Maxwell died May 24 at age 68.

Chapter 25

I am ready–whenever you say
I may begin.

In negotiations with New Albany, Indiana publisher and bookseller John R. Nunemacher, Baynard wrote on August 27, 1855, "I returned the 25th from a Musical Convention and found your two letters. The copy has not yet reached me." The revisions of the 1843 edition of *The New Purchase* were in progress and the publisher was given suggestions for illustrations. Hall promised "grand reviews" from friend George Bush and Alexander Wilson, an editor of *The Brooklyn Daily Times*. Another good review might be gained from David M. Stone, editor-publisher of the (New York) *Journal of Commerce*, also a personal friend. Dr. Robert Davidson supplied his "favorable opinion." Appletons, the New York publisher of the original book, transferred the copyright to the author.

Nunemacher suggested a new title shortened

from the original to *The New Purchase or Early Years in the Far West*. The original two volumes were to be combined into one. Baynard, in keeping with publishers' hopes that authors bring their own and many readers, suggested, "The Wynkoop Brothers Booksellers and Stationers, Syracuse, New York told me last winter when I lectured there they would be happy to aid in the sale...they greatly prize the work." From Hall's letters it can be speculated that Nunemacher approached him in regard to a reprint of the book; although the author may have been fishing for a small-press publisher. The New Albany bookseller must have made some reference to the sales in Indiana because Hall wrote to him, "...you are very far off that very great trouble and inconvenience would attend a publication in my former state—Indiana." In a vague reference to the "Bloomington General," Hall was identifying his old nemesis Jacob Lowe, and quipped to Nunemacher, "by this you may see how true to nature are the pictures and delineations of N. Purchase." (However true the characters in the book were to their human counterparts, the author of *The New Purchase* did not offer to change his *nom de plume* from Robert Carlton, Esq.)

He was trying to work with New York publishers, but they were crying hard times. A deal was struck with Nunemacher that was satisfactory to both including Hall's wish to crop some references to Dr. Wylie and "some passages and words here and there that really mar the work," and he admitted there were passages of which he was ashamed. He added, "If we print here, I am to review and condense into one volume which may retail for $1.25 or even $1.00 per copy." Hall asked for a dozen wholesale copies for himself, and a half-dozen complimentary books, as had been arrangements with other publishers; the free copies he reserved as keepsakes for his children. A key to the fictitious names of characters and places in *The New Purchase* was sent, not totally complete, with the *caveat,* "We must not forget the law of 'libel'." The month of August was a flurry of activity and marked the hoped-for rebirth of the book. (Hall regretted the loss of a little household notebook in which the family had pasted clippings of all the notices of the 1843 edition that could be found, but that small scrapbook is among the Nunemacher papers in the Indiana University Archives.)

The August 17, 1855 issue of *The Daily Journal* of Indianapolis carried an article signed by Governor Joseph A. Wright announcing that the American Colonization Society expected to dispatch a,

> ...vessel well provided with accommodations for emigrants from Baltimore on the first day of November... Persons of color living in this state wishing to emigrate will be transported from Baltimore and sustained for six months after reaching Liberia, at the expense of the state; and each family, or single person without a family, will be

furnished with a tract of land sufficient for their support free of charge.

The New York Times reported January 22, 1853 that the Colonization Society had elected vice-presidents; the name of Joseph Wright, Indiana, was included among them.

While emigrants had to make their own way to Baltimore and pay for their own goods and implements, the accommodations in Liberia for their acclimation "are adequate to the wants of all who will be sent by the Society." The complete article was signed by Joseph A. Wright as President of the Board of Colonization of the State of Indiana. Did this charter student of Baynard Hall at the Indiana Seminary read *Frank Freeman;* did Professor Hall keep up with the accomplishments of the boy called Henry in *The New Purchase,* the boy who dug a well, retrieved the cow, built the college fires and rang its bell, and became Indiana's 10th governor?

Baynard had called on a young and ambitious New York artist, William Momberger, just about the same age as the deceased Rush Hall. The Frankfort, Germany native had been in the United States only seven years and was destined to make a name for himself as an illustrator. By the Civil War years he was producing art for the engravings of historic events and celebrated people. Hall found Momberger "for many reasons to do better and cheaper" than another illustrator being considered, and not a master of English, but a man of high character. Bustling about overseeing the illustrations, editing and proofreading, and promoting the future sales any way he could, Hall also had John Young distribute circulars in New Jersey. The business with the book was carried out in addition to Rev. Hall preaching at the Dutch Reformed Church and teaching five hours every day but Saturday.

Inquiring of Nunemacher about illustrations, Baynard asked, "How would the 'phiz' of Robert Carlton Esq. do for an 'ornament' and illustration?" In an undated, unaddressed letter, he remarked, "the Phiz is better looking now than when we were a youth. I have two Daguerrotypes, but we can easily be done..." In October, he wrote that he was going to Brady to sit for a portrait. At that time Matthew Brady's New York studio was an easy trip for Hall and Brady had gone from daguerreotypes to photographs. Momberger showed Hall how his portrait could be done on wood "just as well as on steel and cost no more or very little beyond the others." The illustrator offered "to put in the Portrait in the fine style for $25." But no picture of Baynard Hall appeared in the book.

He wrote, "I think Momberger in order to 'go down to posterity' with us, will be willing in subsequent bargains between you and him, to alter engravings, etc. He is a gentleman you will like." The pictures chosen for the new *New Purchase* were Old Dick and the bark mill, Rev. Mizraim Ham in mimicry of David and Goliath at the camp meeting, and a portrayal of Paris C. Dunning, Indiana's ninth governor, as a Hoosier lad dashing into White River to escape Hunting Shirt Andy.

The whole is my life for about 8 years and almost every thing in the Work is literally true.

"The book is virtually Fact" (underlined), stated its author in a letter listing revisions, comments, and some actual names of people and places in *The New Purchase.* "The book is a kind of classic in Indiana," he wrote,

> …and is cherished as a pet—and a cheaper edition than the first would sell there extensively. The first (one thousand) sold for $1.50 and sold off in a few weeks. Although the Work appeared in the midst of the Cheap literature age, and sold high, it went off almost immediately—and old Mr. Appleton was so elated that he asked me if he should instantly print a cheap edition of 6,000; I consented, but about this time he died; and as the work was not stereotyped, his sons did not re-print.

Walt Whitman's first *Leaves of Grass* appeared, self-published, with a preface and a dozen untitled poems. In addition, Henry Ward Beecher, Baynard with tongue-in-cheek remarked, "had published the last of the first and most wonderful books in the World!—as every book has been called for many years. At this moment there is a dead calm in the book line, and we could not have a more favorable moment to appear." Always thinking of possible networking, Baynard asked if Dr. Maxwell and Austin Seward were living. "Will not the several Doctors take interest in the book...Bloomington I suppose is wholly changed. James Maxwell Esq. of Grand Gulph was a favorite pupil—he is named in the book as 'the Nevy' in the Indian scene. He could write a review down there." General William McCalla of Washington, Col. Wilmar in the book, requested a copy and could be used to approach the people of the capital. According to Hall, McCalla had bought, read, and approved of the first edition.

Professor George Bush and Presbyterian clergyman and educator, Dr. John Maclean, Jr., President of the College of New Jersey, both advised Hall to omit the Wylie controversy. Dr. Maclean had been Baynard's classmate at the College of New Jersey and Princeton Theological. Hall, juggling page numbers, estimated the new edition to have 450 to 460 pages; the 1843 volumes totaled 616. He advised Nunemacher, "I will keep a look out... and see that something shall fill up, and if possible Bloduplex reduced." The statement suggests that there was lingering resistance to completely removing disparaging references to Dr. Wylie.

The letter from Dr. Robert Davidson was a boon to the book's authenticity.

"You do me the honor to request my opinion of *The New Purchase*...I read it many years ago while residing in the

West and then thought it...a piquant and truthful portraiture of life in the West. The book was read aloud in my family, and we laughed and cried over it alternately."

Professor Bush reported to Hall that Caroline Kirkland, a prolific and popular author, had commented, "Your friend may write what he pleases, but he can never write a work like The New Purchase if he writes one hundred years."

A Philadelphia bookseller ordered a hundred copies from Nunemacher, "if they could be purchased at 75 cents per copy on six months credit." He wrote, "One of us, Alfred Martien, read the book many years ago and well remembers the pleasure it afforded." Hall told Nunemacher that he had no doubt Scribner would take a large number of copies at the special reduction prepared in relation to Hall's friends. "Perhaps if the book takes—we can get up a Key that will sell well, say about one hundred pages, and sell for 50 cents. Please present in my name a Copy of N.P. To Mr. Austin Seward—but not till Mr. S Carlton has sold his 500."

In the preface of the new and improved edition, Hall translated the Latin phrase from his 1843 preface: *Alter et idem. Per multas aditum sibi saepe figuras reperrit* as meaning "pretty much of a muchness, or in better Saxon—Six of one and half a dozen of the other." The other lines he rendered as "being crafty he catches with guile," and adds, "...these are the *freest* translation we are at liberty to give." However, a rank amateur translator from high school Latin might see it as saying: An old and familiar story done up in a cunning and new image; but Professor Hall of classical languages might disagree. Hall, with a literary wink, enjoyed having a joke on his readers.

In his promotion mode, Baynard boasted, "All say the work is unrivaled in its way." Some of his twentieth century critics, looking only at the 1843 edition, agreed, calling its author a smart aleck, complaining of his cumbersome writing, but the most stinging sling and arrow of all—labeling it fiction! In fairness some later observers of *The New Purchase* have taken a deeper look and have seen its intrinsic worth. Dr. George Cheever, another politically minded, respected, and outspoken clergyman, promised a letter to be published in *The Independent,* a religion journal; but, Hall snapped, "*The Presbyterian* takes no notice of us and never did," with underlining.

In mid-December, James Brewer, a banker friend in Troy, New York wrote,

…you say the New Purchase is out. It is strange that I can not get hold of it. I have sent for it three times but all in vain. I have seen neither advertisement nor notice in any paper or periodical. I think that proper means are not taken to get the work before the public?

Baynard wrote to Nunemacher, "Several of my personal friends say they cannot find the Book at the Stores. One or two say we have committed an error in not having the Book announced in Large Letters before the doors of the Bookseller...," and then in another terse letter, "Some things all say should be done and immediately...or we shall suffer disappointment here."

By July, a letter to Nunemacher begins, "I am very sorry our Book appears to be dead." He continued,

> Of course I regret it on my own account, but honestly I sincerely regret it on your account, for I wished you might pocket something handsome for your labor and enterprise. I should be glad to know the worst if you can find spirits enough to favor me with a letter. I could write an ironical and bitter defense of Romanism.

Suggesting such an editorial is a sad commentary on Hall's almost desperate state. He had ridiculed the Pope in print, and the Know Nothing Party with its anti-Catholic bigotry was a force; but he asked,

> Would such a thing take? How would you like to publish? We are all jogging along slowly—but are not likely to be among the millionaires. P.S. Could you sell out to Derby or some publishing firm—I would be willing to take a certain sum in such case and allow such publisher to keep all he can get.

broad and general, and those words are signs and symptoms rather than cause. The obituary concluded, "It is painful to know that his closing days were embittered by great anxiety and the serious pressure of adversity." Words that leave only guesswork. Dr. Robert Sample wrote, "In a letter received from him a few years before his death, he says, 'I am very poor; am nearly sixty years of age, I have buried six children, have three left. Have had a very sorrowful life and am very melancholy and sad now. I feel that sorrow will bring me prematurely to the grave.'" Those morose words were written before the death of daughter Edistina.

Less than 13 months after her father's death, Carolina Baynard Hall, with the lovely voice who sang in Dr. George Cheever's Church of the Puritans, died of tuberculosis in the Brooklyn home on February 2. She was 25. On July 24, Aunt Martha Doughty died there at 91. Mary Ann said goodbye to her last, the one who had lived the longest, Holmes Baynard Hall, 33, dead September 29 of typhoid fever. Mary Ann Young Hall, the mother of nine who traveled through and shared with her husband what was almost a Job-like existence, died November 10 at the age of 68, also of typhoid. She may have lived her adult life and suffered along with the creative and brilliant victim of a bipolar illness. Mercifully for Baynard, he did not survive to see their line extinguished.

The family plot in the Cemetery of the Evergreens is quite large, larger than needed for the eight graves there. The lots are seven feet long and are fronted by a paved street. They border an old bridle path in burial grounds that now hold the remains of over 600,000 people. It is a beautiful spot, easily accessible, except there will never be visits by descendants of Baynard and Mary Ann Hall. "Aunt Doughty," the simple inscription on one monument tells little, says much. But their lives are marked by something more lasting than white marble stones, because...*Words are things.*

Epilogue

Brooklyn June l5th 1863 (To Elinor Reed)
My dear Sister,
I do not owe you a letter, but what is that between you and me? We have been getting our likenesses taken and I thought it would not do to enclose the cartes de visites without saying something in the blank paper—if it is only how do you do?

We have had a very pleasant visit from W. Williams and Josiah. I hope by this time the latter has fairly recovered the use of his leg. They no doubt have reached home and are enjoying the society of loved ones made dearer by a long and anxious absence.

John Young gave us a surprise visit on yesterday. He has a leave of absence for fifteen days. His title now is Major. He goes from here directly to Saint John Missouri to see his Father's and Brother's families. He will take Etty to school to Terre Haute Ind. and may possibly give Mr. Williams a flying visit, but his time is so limited that it is rather doubtful.

We are jogging on pretty much as usual. Aunt is better, but of course very feeble. She sits up part of every day, has a good appetite, but is very deaf from cold as we suppose, but her age has no doubt something to do with it.

Carolina is much better and we hope with care she will become quite healthy.

You must answer my letter which brought you some time since in my debt.

I'll send their love with that of your sister.

Martha

PS You may be able to recognize Aunt's picture and perhaps mine. Sister Mary will send you one when she can have some taken to her liking. Give our love to Ann and all the children. Please send one of each of these pictures to Ann.

The year 1864 was unparalleled. Within ten months, there had been four deaths in the house of Baynard Rush Hall, deceased.

In her Will, Martha Morris Young named her sister Elinor Reed and brother John as survivors; Elinor in Putnam County in Indiana, and John Morris Young in Missouri, but she designated as her one and only heir, Sarah M.F. Scott, who had lived with the family. Martha died November 14, 1866 in the Brooklyn house. Martha, born on her sister Mary's birthday, had spent her almost 64 years always within the shelter of her family. In 1867, the day before Baynard Hall's birthday, John Hopkins Harney died in Kentucky after a career as editor-publisher of *The Louisville Democrat*, and president of colleges that had merged into the University of Louisville.

Elinor Reed, the last of those accomplished, literate women, died at the home of her daughter Lydia Williams in Indiana, May 9, 1869, and was buried in a small family plot on the Williams farm. She is within a half-day's ride, Young settlement time, of her mother's grave in Owen County, but separated in death by many miles from Isaac's grave in Illinois. Son George "Whit" Reed's remains were not found; he has a memorial stone beside his father's. Elinor's daughter Sarah married notable artist William Shackleford who painted a most life-like portrait of Isaac Reed, which hangs in the Presbyterian Church of Greencastle, Indiana.

John Morris Young was in Newton County, Missouri in 1870, age 72, practicing law, a profession for which he was aptly suited. He was living with his son Wallace H. Young and family. John M., Jr. followed in his father's path as a man of varied business interests, including some which took him to Canada. Wallace Young became a successful merchant.

Sarah M.F. Scott inherited the Brooklyn house and the house in Philadelphia. She married Joseph Hadden and lived in Orange County, New York. In 1906, Sarah sold her title to the tract containing 195,840 acres of John Hall's grant for $250.00, the land sold for taxes in 1801.

In 1916, Indiana's centennial year, Princeton University published an edition of Baynard Rush Hall's 1843 *The New Purchase: or Seven and a Half Years in the Far West,* with its original words, and explanations and praise by Dr. James Woodburn of Indiana University, Bloomington, who described it as one of the most valuable documents of early

Indiana history, and an "imperishable" classic.

In 1923, John Inglehart, President of the Southwestern Indiana Historical Society, Evansville, worded two pages about Baynard Rush Hall's *New Purchase*. He did not mince words saying that it represented the bottom layer of social life; that Hall was a bad loser and unable to adjust himself to pioneer life and become a part of it; that the work was cowardly (and criminal) libel.

> The eastern states opposed the addition of new states to the Union, and there existed a fear of the development of an agricultural democracy on account of which theological students like Hall came West in part to preserve the religious and intellectual status quo of these older states. Such a thing was impossible and therefore Hall failed.

"I dare say," said Inglehart,

> ...that the people of Indiana are tired of a third effort to perpetuate this book which never had real public recognition... and for the printing of which no reasonable excuse ever existed....I hope that Princeton University Press managers are satisfied and will give us no more of this kind of missionary literature.

And not the least: The book does "injustice to the better class of people." But, allow the Reverend Dr. Hall to have the last word:

*May I not say...that persons, places, things, etc.
are essentially as you found them?*

—Baynard Rush Hall, *The New Purchase...*,
Preface, 1843

End Notes

Abbreviations and fictitious names in the original *The New Purchase:*

BRH: Baynard Rush Hall (Robert Carlton, Charles Clarence, Mr. Merry)

MAH: Mary Ann Young Hall (Mrs. Carlton, Eliza)

IR: Isaac Reed (Rev. James Hillsbury)

JMY: John Morris Young (John Glenville)

TNP: *The New Purchase:* or *Seven and a Half Years in the Far West* (I used the 1916 edition of 1843, unless otherwise designated.) Editions of 1843, 1855, 1916, (1975 a reproduction).

SFE: *Something for Every Body: Gleaned in The Old Purchase, from Fields Often Reaped,* 1846

TAS: *Teaching a Science: The Teacher as Artist,* 1848

FF: *Frank Freeman's Barber Shop: A Tale,* 1852

TCT: Isaac Reed's *The Christian Traveler,* 1828

Chapter quotes are all Baynard Hall words, unabashedly taken out of context, from different sources, not particularly applicable to the theme of the chapters, but his words. When information is repeated in BRH or other works, I have sometimes inserted only one reference. To document every fact would create more pages than the biography itself; I have not done that. A complete bibliography would also require an inordinate amount of pages. Many references are for further reading, or require readers to do their own Google searches. I confess to breaking another rule: beginning a story with the weather!

Preface:

1. "Said to be entertaining," BRH in 1855 questionnaire from Union College, Union College Alumni Records, Schaffer Library, Schenectady, New York. Previous lines are this author's.

2. Nicholson: "A Reader's Notes," *The Indianapolis Star,* April 3, 1917, p. 8.

3. Banta: *Hoosier Caravan: A Treasury of Indiana Life and Lore,* selected, with comment, by R. E. Banta, Indiana University Press, 1975, p. 153, 154.

4. "dialogue with thy shadow" from "Timon of Athens," Shakespeare, Scene II, Act II.

5. *George Washington, The Image and the Man,* W. E. Woodward, Boni and Liveright, New York, 1926, p. 166.

6. phrenology: determining traits by structure of the skull.

Chapter 1: "Tadpole state..." *FF,* p. 58.

1. Washington quote: Jackson, Donald and Twohig, Dorothy, eds., *The Diaries of George Washington,* University Press of Virginia, Charlottesville, 1979, Vol. 6, p. 279.

2. Turner's Lane: From BRH response to Union College questionnaire, 1855, copy from Union College alumni records. Books about colonial and post-revolution Philadelphia abound. Recommended: Kelley, Joseph J., *Life and Times in Colonial Philadelphia,* Stackpole Books, Harrisburg, Pa., 1973; Shackleton, Robert,*The Book of Philadelphia,* The Penn Publishing Co., Philadelphia, 1918; *Watson's Annals of Philadelphia and Pennsylvania,* Penn State Digital Bookshelf, Watson, John F. 1857; various articles found in *The Pennsylvania Magazine of History,* by Pennsylvania Historical Society, and others online.

3. Some sources say Dr. John Hall was on Washington's staff; I could find nothing to document that the doctor served in that capacity.

4. Dr. Rush: Biographies of Dr. Rush are many; autobiographical material from Corner, George W., ed., *The Autobiography of Benjamin Rush, Travels through Life together with his Commonplace Book for 1789-1813,* published for the American Philosophical Society by Princeton University Press, 1948, Princeton, New Jersey, (Dr. Rush tells he's entertained most of the Continental Congress at his table, p.110.) Entry of Dr. Hall's death,

Commonplace Book, p. 320. Butterfield, L. H., ed., *Letters of Benjamin Rush,* Vol. 1, 1761–1792, published for the American Philosophical Society by Princeton University Press, 1951. (See these works for Dr. Rush's family.) Dr. Elisha Hall's letter about Mary Washington's cancer, *ibid.,* p. 518–519. John and Elisha Hall had an older brother Joseph who was a physician in the Revolution. See Note 5, Chapter 2.

5. Dr. John Hall's Will is online via two sources, but I obtained photocopies of the Will and estate inventory in order to see original and complete details; from Philadelphia County records, Philadelphia, Pa. "Plate" mentioned in the Will refers to plated dinnerware or utensils.

6. Pine Barren lands from John Hall Papers, and documents prepared for Dr. Hall, Georgia Historical Society, Savannah. Also Union College questionnaire, 1855, regarding land speculators.

7. Dr. Hall's estate inventory, above; in Dr. Rush's Memorandum Book, 19, American Philosophical Society; Dr. Rush's accounts for Baynard Hall, p.70–73. (1807–1811).

8. "The dear old Negro woman..." (Daphne Peterson), *SFE* p. 84–87; Daphne as "free black woman," in Dr. Rush's Memorandum Book, 1806: pp. 54, 55, 82, 83.

9. bankruptcy: Act of 1800 Bank Records, U.S. District Court for the Eastern District of Pennsylvania, 1800–1806, M. 993; Richard Hall #196, Peter Conway #197.

10. 1795 land grants: A history of the land grant proceedings is from a quiet title suit: bulk.resource.org/courts.gov., online, a legal opinion from the lawsuit of Richmond Cedar Works v. Pittsburgh Land and Lumber Co. et al., District Court, E.D. North Carolina, December 11, 1916; also Hyde County, North Carolina recorder's office, Swan Quarter, North Carolina, Deed Book Z, p. 353, seven pages; also Tyrrell County, North Carolina Register of Deeds, Columbia, North Carolina, Deed Book 66, p. 250 and Book 79, p. 343. BRH, *TNP*, 13–14. In a final decree in the quieting of title, September 10, 1925, the United States sued Richmond Cedar Works, University of North Carolina, heirs at law of Baynard and Mary Ann Hall, Martha M. Young, John Wyatt and Harriett Hawkins... Dr. Hall's grant included islands, Great Swan Quarter and Great Judico Marshes. Deed dated October 21, 1841 states that 14,160 acres had been previously granted out of No. 317, the first of Dr. Hall's original five tracts, (Z, p.353 above). 1927 document in Tyrrell County Register of Deeds records from District Court of the U.S. for the

Eastern District of North Carolina.

Chapter 2: "My mother's family..." Union College questionnaire, 1855.

1. "more malignant," Butterfield, L.H., *Letters of Benjamin Rush,* Vol. 2, 1793–1813, p. 807.

2. Yellow Fever in Philadelphia: J.H. Powell, *Bring Out Your Dead,* University of Pennsylvania Press, 1949. Jim Murphy, *An American Plague,* Clarion Books, New York, 2003. Other plague years found in Rush letters, autobiography and almost any work dealing with Dr. Rush and Philadelphia. See also Billy G. Smith's *"The Lower Sort," Philadelphia's Laboring People, 1750-1800,* Cornell University Press, 1990; David F. Hawke's *Benjamin Rush, Revolutionary Gadfly*, Bobbs-Merrill, 1971. Also articles online.

3. Elizabeth Hall, Dr. John Hall co-sign deed, dated May 14, 1798; 722 acres in Virginia, witnessed by Bernard Webb and Peter Conway; *Virginia County Land Records, Spotsylvania County,* 1721–1800, Vol. 1, edited by William Armstrong Crozier.

4. Baynard and Grimball genealogies: *The South Carolina Historical and Genealogical Magazine,* Vol. 23, January 1922 and April 1922. Also Porcher, Richard

Dwight and Sarah Flick, *The Story of Sea Island Cotton,* Wyrick & Company, Charleston, 2005. Materials from the South Carolina Room, Charleston Public Library, Charleston, South Carolina. Also, Hasell, Annie Baynard Simons, *Baynard: An Ancient Family Bearing Arms, a compilation, 1972;* digitized online, but I own two copies of the original book, one from rare book dealer, another from a thrift store. Diligent search did not find current copyright owner. BRH may have lodged with first cousins Ephraim M. Baynard or Princeton graduate William Grimball Baynard on his South Carolina trips.

5. Rush, Hall genealogies: Butterfield, Vol. 1, p. 518–19. Corner, *Autobiography of Benjamin Rush...;* also see Pleasants, Dr. J. Hall, "Hall Family," p. 381–382, *Maryland Historical Magazine,* December 1913, and Johnson, Christopher, "Hall Family of Calvert County," in *Maryland Historical Magazine,* p. 291–298, September 1913. Also see BRH document for Union College, 1855.

6. Dr. Rush's children: Butterfield, Vol. 2, p. 834.

7. BRH's maternal uncles' letter to Dr. Rush in Hasell's book of Baynard genealogy, p. 151, 152; copy of original letter in

possession of the South Carolina Historical
Society, Charleston; Uncle William
Baynard died in 1802. BRH, *TNP*, p.14.
Burials in Presbyterian Cemetery, Edisto
Island, South Carolina. "&C." is an archaic
symbol for *etcetera.*

8. Dr. Rush's Memorandum Book for BRH:
Rhodes and Otis and uncles' payments
listed, p. 71.

9. "dishonest agents, claims to land, did
not need their recognition," BRH, *TNP*,
p.13,14.

10. "Is this Miss Betsey's son?" *SFE*, p.85.

11. mother: SFE, p. 74-76.

12. Edisto Island: See Spencer, Charles, *Edisto
Island 1663 to 1860,* The History Press,
Charleston, South Carolina, 2008.

13. "eight or nine children," BRH stated in
the Union College questionnaire that he
was the 10th child; unlikely if his parents
married in 1788 and he was born in
January, l798. He might have been his
mother's 10th pregnancy if there was a
child before her marriage to Dr. Hall. *SFE*,
p.85. Others may include stillbirths.

14. Hall–Baynard marriages: Marriages
of Chatham County, Georgia in Deed
Books 1785–1852; John Hall marries
Elizabeth Ann Elliott, widow of Thomas

Elliott, March 1788, F. 65–68, from
Georgia Historical Society, Savannah.
Also, Holcomb, Brent H., *South Carolina
Marriages 1800-1820,* Genealogy
Publishing Co., Baltimore, 1981. No
marriage record could be found for
Thomas Elliott and Elizabeth Ann Baynard
in South Carolina or Georgia records.

15. Notice of administration: Legal notice
of Dr. Hall for letters of administration
of estate of Thomas Elliott, deceased,
Georgia Gazette, September 5, 1789. No
subsequent records regarding the estate
of Thomas Elliott appear to exist in county
records.

16. Will of Thomas Elliott: Will Book C,
*Abstracts of Wills Chatham County,
Georgia* 1773–1817, abstracted and
compiled by Mabel Freeman LaFar,
Carolina Price Wilson; National Genealogy
Society, Washington D.C., 1962. Drayton
information in collection of South Carolina
Room, Charleston Public Library, The
South Carolina Royal Council, 1720–1763,
Vol. 18, No. 3, p. 373–392, *William and
Mary Quarterly.* Spanish dollar (or piece-
of-eight) explained by Lou Jordan, Director
of Rare Books and Special Collections,
University of Notre Dame, Fellow of
the American Numismatic Society and
Associate Editor of *The Colonial Newsletter.*

17. Will of William Baynard, Edisto Island, Province of South Carolina, Will Record 15, p. 399; Will of Mrs. William (Elizabeth) Baynard, Edisto Island, etc., Will Record 15, p. 525; copies in South Carolina Room, Charleston Public Library. A recently published genealogy of the Baynards completely omits the name of Elizabeth Baynard Hall, listing the children of William and Elizabeth as Thomas and William only.

18. trips south: *SFE,* p. 85. Trip to Edisto Island "previous winter" = 1819. In IR, *TCT,* May 1820.

19. "wild oats," *SFE,* p.77.

20. "a mother's prayer," *ibid.,* p.76.

21. "Enter their churches...," *FF,* p.114.

22. Daphne Peterson: *SFE,* p.84–87.

23. slavery: *ibid.,* p.55–56. Read *FF* in its entirety to glean BRH's purpose and methods. Readers have to tread through distractions, but it contains some autobiographical material.

24. Daphne's death: Philadelphia Death Records, cause: dysentery, age 94, burial First Baptist Cemetery. Will recorded in Book 8, folio 47; inventory appraised and dated August 1, 1823. In an accounting of the estate in 1825, "household furniture

since ascertained as not belonging to the estate."

Chapter 3: "The End of Education is the Power or Art of Thinking." *TAS*, p 56.

1. early education of BRH: Union College questionnaire, Dr. Rush's Memorandum Book.

2. American Whig and Cliosophic Societies: *Prodesse Quam Conspici: An Oration Delivered June 1852,* published by Charles Scribner, New York, 1852.

3. Union College: BRH academic record from Union College; Union University Centennial Catalog, 1795–1895, printed in Troy, N.Y., 1895; correspondence from M. DesChamps, Archives Specialist, Schaffer Library, Union College, Schenectady, New York.

4. College of New Jersey (Princeton) and Princeton Theological Seminary: Records from Seeley G. Mudd Manuscript Library, Princeton University, Princeton, New Jersey; Archives and Special Collections of Princeton Theological Seminary and 1855 Union College questionnaire.

5. BRH licensed: Place and date given in lecture by Rev. Robert Sample, May 1866; Bedford Presbyterian Church records and

papers, Pioneer Library, Bedford County Historical Society, Bedford, Pennsylvania.

6. Eliphalet Nott: *Eliphalet Nott,* an abridgement of the biography by Codman Hislop, Union College, Schenectady, 1995. An interesting read for educators. Also biography online.

7. Presbyterians: Indiana's Presbyterian history can be found in *Contributions to The Early History of the Presbyterian Church in Indiana,* Hanford A. Edson, Winona Publishing, 1898; *Hoosier Zion,* L.C. Rudolph, Yale University Press, 1963; and the *History of Hanover College,* A.Y. Moore, the Hollenbeck Press, Indianapolis, 1900, also "Presbyterianism on the Frontiers," Rev. Joseph F. Tuttle, D.D., President, Wabash College, reprinted online from *The Presbyterian Quarterly and Princeton Review,* 1877. L.C. Rudolph also produced an encyclopedic *Hoosier Faiths: A History of Indiana Churches & Religious Groups,* Indiana University Press, 1995.

Chapter 4: "I loved as they say one can love but once." *FF,* p.156.

1. Holmes family: Philadelphia census, directories, and Will records; deed record from Thomas and John Penn, sons of

William Penn to Nicholas Young, Sr.,
shipjoiner, March l3, 1773; marriage
records of Second Presbyterian Church;
birth and baptismal records . Basic
genealogical research by descendants
Karen Kotlarchik and Raymond Holmes,
also Priscilla Normandy Greenwood.
My sources are too lengthy to cite here.
Interested genealogists know to consult
Ancestry.com. The Holmes men are given
the fictitious name "Seymour" by BRH.
The original name appears to be Holme,
but many contemporary documents were
signed as Holmes.

2.   Hall–Young marriage: Isaac Reed, *TCT*,
diary entry for spring of 1820 writes
of Mary Ann and Baynard's marriage.
BRH stated marriage was in 1821, but
no marriage record has been located in
Kentucky; nor can Rev. Samuel Kelsey
Nelson's records be found. Judging by the
age of their first child at his death, 1820 is
the year.

3.   courtship: *TNP*, p. 14, 90. *FF*, p. 156:
"We were schoolmates and companions
in childhood...we were always lovers," I
believe is reflective of BRH and MAH
relationship.

4.   Ann Holme Young: *TCT*, April 1826 entry,
and *TNP*, p. 255–257.

5. family's reversal of fortune: *TNP*, p. 89, 90.

6. Daniel Jaudon: Sellers, Edwin J., *Jaudon Family of Pennsylvania*, Philadelphia, 1926. Katie Ives of the Jaudon family. Location of seminary in 1825 Philadelphia Directory.

7. "...folk that knew all about three-story houses in Philadelphia...." *TNP*, p.93.

8. Rabb, Kate Milner, Indiana author, from her "Hoosier Listening Post" column in *The Indianapolis Star* newspaper, October 30, 1929. I was unable to identify Margaret Carlisle. Recommended: *Worthy Partner: The Papers of Martha Washington*, compiled by Joseph E. Fields, Greenwood Press, Westport, Conn., 1994. Robert and Martha Holmes Doughty lived in Elfreth's Alley row houses, many of which were occupied by craftsmen as homes and shops, and are desirable places of residence today.

9. Washingtons' home was at 190 Market Street. The Washingtons' activities in Philadelphia are documented in almost any biography of George and/or Martha. Particularly readable are Blair Nailes' *Martha's Husband: An Informal Portrait of George Washington*, McGraw-Hill, New York, 1951; James Thomas Flexner's *Washington: The Indispensable Man*, Little, Brown and Company, Boston and Toronto, 1969; and Patricia Brady's *Martha*

Washington: An American Life, Viking Penguin, 2005. Correspondence with Edward Lawler, Jr. of the Independence Hall Association of Philadelphia, and Historical Society of Pennsylvania. Articles in *Pennsylvania Magazine of History*, Philadelphia articles online.

10. Holmes family: see Chapter 4, note 1. Aunt Doughty: *TNP*, p.165, 166.

11. Aunt Doughty as "Kitty Littleton," *ibid.*, p. 317. Martha Holmes Doughty's husband Robert Doughty, Jr. was a cousin of Philadelphia natives and brothers William Doughty, ship designer, and Thomas T. Doughty, Hudson River artist and contemporary of BRH, who lived at one time in Dutchess County, New York. See http://www.cowaro.com/Genealogy/Surname_file/Young.html#LB_01.

Chapter 5: "Civilized man, and he only, turns wastes into verdure...," from speech 1852, "Prodesse quam Conspici," at College of New Jersey, printed by Charles Scribner, New York, 1852.

1. Centre College: Founded in 1819, the college thrives today. The home in which the Halls and probably the Reeds were married no longer exists. See IR, *TCT*.

2. Williamson Dunn and David H. Maxwell:

Woollen, William W., *Biographical and Historical Sketches of Early Indiana,* Hammond & Co., Indianapolis, 1883; also see "Sketch of Dr. David H. Maxwell," by Louise Maxwell, *The Indiana Magazine of History,* Vol. 8, No. 3, September 1912. Moore, A. Y. *History of Hanover College,* Blanchard, Charles, ed., *History of Morgan, Monroe and Brown Counties, Indiana,* 1884. Williamson Dunn donated land for Wabash College at Crawfordsville. Dr. Maxwell's wife Mary was a sister of Williamson Dunn. Dr. Maxwell appears in all histories of Indiana University; Dunn in Indiana histories due to his many contributions. BRH names him Mr. Blank in *TNP,* the story of the Tippecanoe visit. Dunn is also in any history of Indiana Presbyterianism. Dr. Maxwell's obituary, *Bloomington Newsletter,* June 10, 1854; microfilm, Indiana State Library, Indianapolis, and *Maxwell History and Genealogy,* Florence Houston, et al., C. E. Pauley and Co., Indianapolis, 1916. Dr. Maxwell was an Indiana legislator many years. Also Blanchard's *History of Owen County,* 1844, p. 553, Dunn and Maxwell in War of 1812.

3. Princeton Theological Degree: Princeton Theological Seminary Special Collections, and *TNP,* p. 516, tuition paid.

4. Reeds' first child: Reed's autobiography and *TCT*, also family records. Isaac Reed's unedited autobiography in a typed form was given to me from the Greencastle, Indiana Presbyterian Church by Jane Williams, church secretary; that will be referred to as "autobiography." (An article on the Reeds using this material was published in the *Indiana Magazine of History,* September 1982, by Donald E. Thompson and Lorna Lutes Sylvester who wrote that IR bought a farm in Owen County. This "farm," not a cleared or productive farm for many years, was a densely forested area.) Also, Krys Douglas, Holmes-Reed descendant via Lydia Ann Lapsley Reed, provided material.

5. Holmes, Youngs and Reeds to Owen County: *TCT; TNP,* p. 91. Bethany Presbyterian Church records. Owen County Deed Records, courthouse, Spencer, Indiana; U.S. Bureau of Land Management Records showing original patents.

6. Halls' children: Figuring the conception and birth of John Hall, infant, from Second Presbyterian Church of Philadelphia burial records, Peter Lesley, sexton; date and age, and the same process for second child, a daughter, first name not recorded. J.C. Otto signed a document that the girl died

January 29; Philadelphia Department of Archives. No baptismal records found.

7. John Young, merchant and surveyor: *TNP*, chapters 23, 24, and 25 are devoted to brother-in-law John Morris Young's adventures before the Owen settlement. John is called "Glenville," by BRH, hence the Glenville settlement. These chapters digressing from Hall's story of life in Owen County are confusing to the reader.

8. "They...tasted...the wormwood of affliction's cup." *TNP*, p.319.

9. trip south: *ibid.*

10. deaths of children: *ibid.* Also see note 6 above.

Chapter 6: "The time of the journey was late April." *TNP*, p. 19, 48.

1. Colonel Wilmar: General John Moore McCalla, Virginia Historical Society, *Guide to African American Manuscripts. #480*, Microfilm reel C119, correspondence 1841–50, concerns American Colonization Society, arrangements for emigrants to Liberia, mentions difficulties collecting money from local members of the American party for the Washington Monument Fund because so many members are secret abolitionists; also http:/ www.congressionalcemetery.org/Research/

Rosters/VeteransWar_1812.pdf. General McCalla, born near Lexington, Kentucky, was a promoter of BRH's 1855 ed. of *TNP* (although much of the story about Colonel Wilmar was omitted from the revised edition). BRH, undated letter to publisher Nunemacher. BRH may have gained inspiration and information from General McCalla for *Frank Freeman*.

2. stage trip: The journey covers the first 34 pages of *TNP*. By assuming identities of Charles Clarence *and* Robert Carlton, BRH is telescoping two journeys—with and without Mary Ann, one of his literary devices.

3. breakfast: The breakfast even grislier than my excerpt, *ibid.*, p.23.

4. voyage: steamboats, arks..., keelboats, etc. *TNP*, Chapters 8 and 9, p.36–49.

5. "The ethereal floated...," *ibid.*, p.47.

6. Maysville, *ibid.*, p. 48.

7. "buttermilk, spouty....snaggy land, *ibid.*, 49; "slashy" is a swampy thicket, according to Britannica, although "slash" can refer to felled trees and brush.

8. descendants: Lest readers think this author is an elitist, my 3x great-grandfather, a Revolutionary War veteran coming by way of Maryland, Pennsylvania, and Kentucky,

lived just south of Bloomington during Hall's time and lived out his life with his son in Owen County.

9. "From Loo'ville, I allow?" *TNP*, p.53.

10. Miserable cabin, fried chicken, and Big Bean Creek: *ibid.*, p.51–55.

11. French cook: *ibid.*, p.52.

12. Rev. William Parsons: Parsons was the name given by BRH to Presbyterian pastor Rev. William W. Martin whose son Rev. William Alexander Parsons Martin, born 1827, was a missionary to China. William W. Martin served in Indiana 32 years, 24 in the Livonia area. Covell, Ralph R., *W.A.P. Martin, Pioneer of Progress in China;* Christian University Press, 1978. Rudolph, L.C., *Hoosier Zion.*

13. payment of pastors: *TCT,*, entry July 15, 1827; *TNP*, p.59, 121.

Chapter 7: "white population, very sparse, mainly very poor..." *TNP*, p. 63.

1. BRH says for "about eight years," Bloomington was the "center of their orbit." *ibid.* History of Bloomington, see in Blanchard's *History of Morgan, Monroe and Brown Counties.*

2. different: *TNP*, p.61.

3. For a long and colorful description of how Dr. Maxwell was dressed (but in loving terms), "he was a rare jewel," see *TNP*, p. 62, 63; most omitted from my text. Dr. Maxwell was given the fictitious name, "Dr. Sylvan," for his love of the outdoors.

4. trees: *TNP*, pp. 73, 190, 191.

5. "Come then I will introduce our settlement." *TNP*, p. 86.

6. William Payne: Blanchard, *History of Owen County*, 1884, Owen County Historical Society reprint, Spencer, Indiana, 1977, p. 767,771; also Kline, Dixie, *Fact and Folklore of Owen County*, Vol. 2, 1982, p. 28.

7. Robinson: Tom Robertson; Kline, 1982, pp. 30, 31, 58, and *TNP*, p.160.

8. James Mathes: Kline, *ibid.*, p.12,13, and *History of Owen County*, pp. 701,702, 705.

9. Isaac Reed: *TCT* and later autobiography; also *TNP*, chapters 13, 14 tell of the beginning of the Young settlement and the finding of it by the Halls. Reed did not start Bethany Church as recorded in Blanchard's *History of Owen County*, p. 771.

10. Neighbor Sturgis and Squire Brushwood: TNP, p.79, 171. Brushwood identified by Dr. Woodburn as Sturgis Huckberry, a name not found in Owen County

records; and I could not find it in any BRH references. A descendant and early records of the township indicate strongly that these two names are actually Solomon Dunagan, blacksmith and Baptist preacher, who lived in the right place and time to be this character. Hall's key and those names identified by Dr. Woodburn are not entirely correct, but certainty is not possible.

11. Fannie Elssler: *TNP,* p. 78; Austrian ballet dancer who toured the U.S. in 1840–42.

12. "The Hoosier Homespun of Baynard Rush Hall," Dixie Kline, *The Star Magazine, The Indianapolis Star,* November 5, 1978, a brief sketch of BRH and *TNP.*

Chapter 8: "...subdivide two hundred and eighty-nine square feet...", *TNP,* p.94.

1. John Morris Young: *TNP,* p.181–192 are devoted to BRH's brother-in-law.

2. Duff Green: A short biography can be found online; another Kentucky connection.

3. John Young as a Representative: Interesting reading in the volumes of Records of the Indiana House of Representatives, John Young is in volume covering 13th session.

4. Hanover College opened in 1827 in a log cabin; was adopted as a synod school by the

Indiana Presbytery in 1829; see *History of Hanover College.*

5. The Young Settlement: Called "Glenville," in *TNP*, location and description, p.86–89.

6. Scotch carpet: The makeshift room divider was a wool rug.

7. japanned tray: a lacquered tray. George Washington was charged for damage to a japanned waiter (tray) by a landlord in a rental home; p. 300, Shackleton, Robert, *The Book of Philadelphia.*

8. window: Panes of glass were an economic indicator, replacing oiled paper windows. A humorous incident regarding buying and installing panes is related; also talk of half-cents and fipenny bits in *TNP*, p.215–221. I did not include those segments.

9. "I stood in a small copse," is my reverie.

10. Old Dick and the tannery: The venerable horse is introduced, tannery described, *TNP*, p. 100–104.

11. Payne settlement: BRH calls it the Welden settlement; Woodburn's key says the Payne settlement. I believe it is actually the Steele settlement where the Bethany Presbyterians began, March 1820, founded by Rev. J. M. Dickey, Montgomery Township, Owen County; the Paynes were Methodists. *TNP* pp.. 117,123,132. See

meeting, *TNP,* p. 119. Welden Diocese, p. 287, also p. 234, Welden as lay delegate. Paynes in Blanchard's *History of Owen County,* p.773. "revile others...,"*TNP,* p. 66.

12. Aunt Doughty and the guts: *TNP,* p.165, 166. BRH blanked the word guts.

13. hired girls: *ibid.*, pp. 89,103, 166, 263.

14. livelong, blessed day (livelong, bless-ed): *ibid.*, p.151 and my grandmother, Bess Rice.

15. wedding: Perhaps Susan Asher and James Matlock in 1825 or Susannah Brasher (Brasier) and Richard Walters in 1827? See Owen County Marriage Records. Impossible to determine since BRH so muddled his fictitious names and years. Perhaps this too is a combination of nuptial rites as celebrated in The Purchase, and a key in the future may unlock the true identities of the wedding party. I have made a leap of faith in my account of those identities.

16. "a very little stranger...," *TNP,* p. 229.

17. baby arrives: Daughter Elizabeth's birth is in Chapter 29, p. 229, titled as the "second year." Using Elizabeth's death in 1832 at age eight, this places her birth in 1824. I believe she was conceived in Philadelphia before BRH left for the trip south from

which he returned to find his two children deceased in February 1824. The notched stick reference was a favorite of my maternal grandmother.

18. "calomy and jolop": Camomile and jalap were common herbal remedies. Hall uses the common pronunciation of these medicinals.

19. Amasa Joslin: Dr. Joslin is "Professor Pillbox" by BRH's nomenclature; if Dr. J. was four feet, ten inches tall, it is not found elsewhere. He was Spencer, Indiana's first doctor. Dr. Joslin appears to have filled in someone's term in the Indiana House of Representatives. Also see Blanchard, *History of Owen County,* and Joslin family file in Owen County Public Library, Spencer, Indiana.

20. childbed convalescence: I have no source to show that Mary Ann Hall kept to her bed after the delivery. Pioneer women usually gave birth and returned to their routines but believing the easterners were of a different constitution, I prefer to give Mary Ann Hall a rest from household labors, as was done in future generations, at least for a while.

21. burial of Elizabeth: Isaac Reed's *The Youth's Book,* 1840. A four-part publication of addresses, poetry, the life and letters

of his daughter Martha, and the "three cousins" section in which he writes of nieces Elizabeth Hall and Martha Sanford (his sister Lydia Reed Sanford's daughter), all of whom died in their youth. These sections were sent to me by a generous descendant from an original copy. Also *TNP,* p. 475–477.

Chapter 9: "The reader will readily perceive a good deal of commonplace..." *SFE,* Preface

1. Uncle John, lay delegates: *TNP,* p. 234, 287.

2. Uncle Tommy, preaching, *ibid.,* p. 147, 148–152.

3. Uncle Tommy's cabin, *ibid.,* pp.168,169,170.

4. Aunt Nancy's venison, *ibid.,* p. 170.

5. Hall's winter activities: *ibid.,* p. 158–60; "skuttles" for the loom in the Woodburn edition is a typographical error: shuttles.

6. fireplace: *ibid.,* p. 161–164.

7. "made the apostles talk," *ibid.,* p.158. Translation is "you Tityrus 'neath a broad beech canopy reclining on the slender oat rehearse your silvan ditties..." from *Vergil Ecologues,* Greenough, J. B., online. A typographical error in "popupholosboio thalasses" should read "poluphloisboio." From Homer, it's "of the loud-roaring sea;"

error not caught in 1843 and 1916 editions. In 1855, it's "poluphlosboio." While BRH is studying and in deep reflection, is he walking the forested banks of White River? Translation of Greek, correspondence with Barbara McManus, Professor of Classics Emerita, College of New Rochelle, New York.

8. "to the day of our death," Hall letter to Wylie, November 6, 1828; President's Records Collection, Wylie C207, Indiana University Archives, Bloomington.

Chapter 10: "Men of science may, indeed, fall into errors." *SFE*, p.156

1. indictment of Dunning and Lowe: Owen County, Indiana Civil Order Book 1, pp. 98, 105; Dunning trial, 125.

2. Deciphering "Hunting Shirt Andy" is an ongoing challenge; there may someday be a "key" found for unlocking this wonderful example of a tale that could have been lost forever, and a missing chapter of local history.

3. Indians: Kline, *Fact & Folklore of Owen County*, 1982, p. 12, 29; Blanchard, *History of Owen County*, p.701. "This Was Once Red Man's Land" (BRH quote), Dixie Kline, in *Spencer Evening World*, Spencer, Indiana, May 24, 1978. Dunn-Maxwell

relative sees tribes migrating, Blanchard's *History of Owen County*, p. 553.

4. Big Fire, Delawares: *History of Owen County*, p. 701. BRH uses "Blue Fire," and in *TNP*, p. 68, and letter to Nunemacher, April 14, 1855, says "Red Fire."

5. Dunning and Lowe, from families who came to Monroe County, Indiana from near Guilford Court House, N.C., at the same time. Blanchard's *History of Morgan, Monroe and Brown Counties*, p. 453; William Lowe's Will, probate records, Monroe County.

6. Hunting Shirt Andy: *TNP*, p. 221–229. Article from *Owen County Journal* newspaper, February 26, 1874, reprints story and adds a preface detailing identities and some circumstances. The incident was well known. His date is wrong, but a Morgan County pioneer related the story, reproduced in *Morgan County History and Genealogy*, Vol. 14, No. 1, Winter 2008. *Journal* article surely mistaken that students were Dr. Jenkins'. See Dr. Maxwell's house, skeleton, *TNP*, p 68. Dr. Jenkins: in "A Hoosier Listening Post," Kate Milner Rabb, *The Indianapolis Star*, March 1, 1926.

7. Bill Roland is John Roland; a John Roland was a commissioner to locate capital of

Iowa, see Territory of Iowa Official Register 1909–10, p. 60, 61. Ben Arnold is Ephraim Goss' son-in-law, Blanchard, *History of Owen County,* p.709. (Jenkins, Freeland, Lowe, Allison, Howe all inter-related families of Monroe, some spilling into Owen County.) Dr. Jenkins, see Kate Raab's "Hoosier Listening Post," note 6 above. Manumission papers by Ephraim Goss, in Washington County, Indiana records; I do not have book and page; date is April 18, 1815; provided by descendant, Debbie Jennings. A typographical error in the 1916 edition, *TNP,* uses "afreed" for afraid. In 1855, it is "afeerd," and I have used that spelling.

8.   Benjamin Fuller: Banta, R. E., *Benjamin Fuller and Some of His Descendants, 1765-1958,* published 1997. Is White-Andy, the second cousin, a clue that someday someone will use to pin "Hunting Shirt Andy" on the actual storyteller?

9.   James Anderson Maxwell: See Indiana University histories, Maxwell family data; and letter of BRH to Nunemacher, August 14, 1855. Not to be confused with James Darwin Maxwell, son of Dr. David H. Maxwell. Nunemacher papers from Indiana University Archives, Bloomington, given by Emma Nunemacher Carlton, daughter of publisher/bookseller John Nunemacher of New Albany, Indiana.

10. Paris Dunning: See biographies. Governor, 1848–1849, succeeded by a BRH student, Joseph Wright. The trial that Dunning interrupted was probably the 1867 Jimmy Johns murder case; Dunning's niece, Mary Dunning Johns, was the widow; see Kline, *Fact & Folklore of Owen County*, Vol. 1, 1976, p. 7–9. Transcripts of that trial were not found in Owen County civil or criminal court records.

11. Dr. Enos Lowe: Biography online, from Andreas' *History of the State of Nebraska.*

    "Black Hawk's Vanished Bones," *The New York Times*, September 25, 1891. Enos, Jacob, and Jesse Lowe (first mayor of Omaha) were sons of William Lowe who was opposed to the Presbyterian faculty and Dr. Maxwell's politics. What finally happened to Black Hawk's remains is another story.

12. Big Fire's remains: Federal Register, Vol. 68, No. 161, August 20, 2003, p. 50189–90. Also correspondence with me from Stacey O. Espenlaub, NAGPRA Coordinator, American Section, University of Pennsylvania Museum of Archaeology & Anthropology, Philadelphia, documenting repatriation of remains to Miami Tribe of Oklahoma with support of the Peoria Tribe of Oklahoma.

Chapter 11 "We were now fully under weigh at Bloomington." *TNP,* p. 263

1. move, girls' school posters: *ibid.,* p. 257 to 265. Hall terms as the third year, Chapter 33. In this chapter he relates how Aunt Doughty is mistaken for his wife and remarks she is just thirty-five years and six months his senior. This is the age difference between Hall and his mother-in-law, Ann Young. Aunt Doughty was 25 years older than Hall. Dr. Maxwell's house, p. 69, 70. On January 26, 1827, a long display ad appears in the *Bloomington Republican* for Mary Hall and Martha Young's school, on microfilm, Indiana State Library.

2. piano: *ibid.,* p. 260: "I set out for Louisville to lay in goods, and also to bring out for our school-purposes, a piano." This refers to their private school, not the seminary.

3. Insidias Cutswell: TNP, p. 273–277 and letter to Nunemacher, August 14, 1855. Insidias is changed to "friend William," p. 257 in the 1855 edition, *TNP.*

4. Old Dick: A fond and final tribute, *TNP,* p. 259.

5. Sarah Reed: Reed family records; Bethany Presbyterian Church records. A comparison of Elinor Reed's handwriting in a letter shows she made the entry of her

children's baptisms in the Bethany Records. Bethany is the oldest still-active, pioneer-founded church in Owen County.

6. sawmill sermon: *TNP,* p. 240, 241; BRH has another persona, "Mr. Merry."

7. John Conner: BRH calls him Mr. Redwhite but keys him as John Conner, Indian agent; the descriptions better fit brother William Conner. An excellent source for the Conners is Charles N. Thompson's *Sons of the Wilderness,* first ed., Indiana Historical Society, 1937; and Conner Prairie Press, Noblesville, Indiana, 1988.

8. Isaac Reed leaving, JMY defeated in clerk's race: *TNP,* p. 286. Debts owed Young and Hall: it seems that at the end of his Bloomington tenure, Hall may have also been helping pay off debts incurred by the mercantile business with his brother-in-law, p.512, 513. I was unable to find any records of the election of the county clerk at that time.

9. Uncle Tommy leaves: *TNP,* p. 286, 287; not knowing his whereabouts, omitted from 1855 edition.

10. Wabash Presbytery: Woodburn's footnote says this was formed in 1822 or 1823, but the date is actually 1825. *TNP,* p. 234, 235; *Hoosier Zion,* p.101.

11. BRH ordained: *The Indiana Gazette,* Bloomington, May 21, 1825, from *The Indianapolis Journal,* April 26. See *History of Hanover College,* A.Y. Morris.

12. Eunice Beecher: *From Dawn to Daylight; or, The Simple Story of a Western Home,* Derby and Jackson, New York, 1859, p. 40.

13. "Proceed we to open the college." *TNP,* p. 322.

14. histories of Indiana University. See note 6.

15. J.M.H. Allison: *History of Owen County* (also an entrepreneur in Greene County); see Allison family file in Owen County Public Library, Spencer, Indiana.

16. post office story: *TNP,* p. 208.

17. seminary opens: *ibid.,* p.319–322. Because the Halls were in Philadelphia in early 1824 having buried two children, they could not have lived in Owen County for some months, moved to Bloomington, and opened the college in April of that year. See also ads for opening college, Chapter 12, and note 7 below. BRH says opened in May.

18. hopeful, first students: *TNP,* p. 323. See note 6, in Chapter 17 notes. The Williamson Dunn and the Maxwell families are to be thanked for helping populate the college!

19. John Harney: IU histories, biographical online, and Harney family data from Linda Harney MacDonald; *TNP,* BRH names him "Prof. Harwood." Letter by Harney: President's Records Collection, Wylie, C207, Indiana University Archives, Bloomington. John Harney, who had a twin sister, Nancy, was a first cousin of William Selby Harney of military notoriety, and a legend in his own time.

20. beginning of Indiana University: See *Indiana University, Its History from 1820, When Founded to 1890,* Theophilus A. Wylie, William. B. Burford, Indianapolis, 1890; *History of Indiana University 1820-1902,* James Albert Woodburn, Indiana University, 1940; *Indiana University: Midwestern Pioneer,* Vol. 1, Thomas D. Clark, Indiana University Press, 1970. Derivative material can be found easily.

Chapter 12: "My mother-in-law had been a very beautiful woman." *TNP,* p. 262

1. Owen County deed records, Recorder's Office, courthouse, Spencer, Indiana.

2. IR, *TCT.*

3. BRH, *TNP,* p. 255–257.

4. "I may look on trees planted in company with others, but we shall never sit together under their shade. *Prodessi,* p .40.

5. endings, beginnings: *TNP*, pp. 257, 286, 287.

6. Reeds, Thomas and Nancy Holmes leave: *TCT* and *TNP*, p. 287.

7. John Holmes admitted to Hanover Presbyterian Church, November 1834, and John Young in May 1835, in John Finley Crowe's record book, Hanover College Archives.

8. *Indiana Gazette*, microfilmed copy badly damaged, of April 1, 1826, says "for the second year." The ad has a start date of March 30; no March 30 issue exists in Indiana State Library collection, Indianapolis.

9. Vincennes meeting: *TNP*, p. 292; Tuttle, p. 23 (see Chapter 3, note 7).

10. sermon at General Assembly, printed by Smith & Bolton, 1827. Indiana State Library, Indianapolis.

11. Robert Bonness and Dan Smith, both of rural Gosport, champions of this research, and among my chief field guides, died while the book was in progress.

Chapter 13 "...in the pell-mell style of history..." *TNP*, p. 333

1. trustees meeting interrupted: *ibid.*, p. 328–334.

2. Dr. Maxwell's editorial: *Gazette,* Bloomington, May 28, 1825.

3. Young-Wallace wedding: Owen County Marriage Records. Another Wallace connection was poet William Ross Wallace (born 1819), a Bloomington and Hanover scholar, close friend of Edgar Allen Poe, and author of "the hand that rocks the cradle is the hand that rules the world." A Margaret Wallace lived near the Halls in Bloomington, with a son between 10 and 15 years of age in 1830; she may be the mother of William Ross Wallace and step-mother of John Harney's wife, Martha. See note 3, Chapter 16. Aletha Wallace may be a part of this family. Woodburn's footnote, 1916 ed., says this was held in a house at the southwest corner of College Avenue and 4th Street, p. 450. See Chapter 16, note 3.

4. Tippecanoe tour: *TNP,* p.334–362.

5. master's degree: Board of Trustees Minutes, September 1827, Miami University Archives, Oxford, Ohio; correspondence from Robert Schmidt, archivist.

6. IR autobiography, family records.

7. Hall baby girl, no name recorded; BRH letter to Wylie, President's Records, Collection C207, Indiana University Archives, Bloomington.

8. "...the glory of Young settlement was fading." *TNP*, p. 314.

9. campaigning: *ibid.*, p. 175–181.

10. John Young sells: Owen County Deed Records, Book 2, p. 202.

11. IR, autobiography; Rush Baynard: Hall's children found and verified through census searches, death records, newspaper items.

12. Christmas, Uncle John injured: *TNP*, p. 314–318.

13. See note 10.

14. "I cried." in *TNP*, p. 318.

Chapter 14: "... is it any wonder Calvinism is on the decline?" *TNP*, p. 377.

1. camp meeting: *ibid.*, p. 364–389.

2. Momberger: letter to Nunemacher, October 6, 1855; Indiana University Archives. The Nunemacher papers are letters regarding 1855 revision of *TNP*.

3. ("Hissin" as a colloquialism for his was often used by my grandmother.) For a "tour" of language, see W.L. McAtee, *Studies in the Vocabularies of Hoosier Authors: Baynard Rush Hall*, printed by the compiler, Chapel Hill, N.C., 1960. Also, Marvin Carmony's *Indiana Dialects in their Historical Setting*, January 1979, constitutes

Indiana Folklore, Vol. 2, No. 3.

4. Hall claims there were at least ten sects in the Monroe County area.

5. Barton Stone and William Armstrong: biographical material online; *TNP,* p.272; also see Name Index to *The Christian Messenger,* September 6, 1827, Monroe County by Ruth E. Browning; http://www. mun.ca/rels/restmov/texts/resources/index/

6. Baby can spell: *TNP,* p. 441–442. Has six children in heaven: p. 423 in 1855 edition., *TNP.* I have used all the actual names in this segment.

Chapter 15: "…a fresh start would be given in its growth." *TNP*, p. 497.

1. Guzzleton barbecue: *ibid.,* pp. 477, 497– 502. The celebration at Gosport is comic relief toward the end of *TNP,* in the midst of BRH writing about the Wylie disputes; but the actual time of the big picnic is impossible to determine. I have by best guess placed it in 1828, in which case it could be associated with John Young's stint as a legislator.

2. Isaac Brasier's distillery: *History of Owen County,* p.708.

3. four friends: Using the key by BRH, Woodburn, and my guesses: *TNP,* p. 501:

James Borland, Peter Batterton; others could be Thomas Ashbrook or Bartlett Asher, local Revolutionary War veterans; Tom Robertson, or neighbor Brasier? (See *Veterans of the American Revolution Who Settled in Owen County*, Dixie Kline Richardson, 1990, Owen County Public Library, Spencer, Indiana). The true identity of "Ashmore" and others named will probably never be known because of BRH forgetfulness or his purposely misleading. In letter to Nunemacher, August 14, 1855, he states, "John Cradock, John Hutson, Mr. Steele were all the real men "named" Hilton, etc." This letter contains most of the identities BRH revealed.

Chapter 16: "The society of Bloomington...." *TNP*, p.55

1. education philosophies: *ibid.*, p. 397.

2. Elinor Catharine Reed: *TCT*, IR autobiography, Reed family records.

3. Young-Wallace wedding: *TNP*, p. 442–45; BRH has this in the "fifth" year. Although she didn't know the names and other particulars, Margaret McCullough, granddaughter of Austin Seward, related the "pig in the window" story in "Pioneer Tales," p.455, (and verified her grandfather

said BRH wrote true stories) in *History of Lawrence and Monroe Counties*, B. F. Bowen & Co., Indianapolis, 1914. John and Aletha's marriage is recorded in Owen County marriage records; the wedding was in Monroe County.

4. D note in alt is the D between G and F above the fifth line of the treble clef, (high).

5. Miss Ladybooks: *ibid.*, p.448, are the Owen girls says Woodburn, *TNP* p. 440, (later Mrs. Irvin Maxwell and Mrs. James Hughes).

6. Peter Batterton: Peter's wife Matilda was the youngest sister of Dr. David Maxwell. Peter was a cabinet maker with a shop on the "corner of main south and east streets," Bloomington: *Indiana Gazette* display ad, January 1, 1825.

7. Young divorce: September 28, 1844 in chancery court, Jefferson County civil records, Clerk's Office, Madison, Indiana. Decree says pending suit advertised in Madison newspaper issues, 1843. Those issues were not found.

8. Hall's age: Both David Banta and Dr. Woodburn cite BRH born in 1793, an error of five years too early. "Good professors as important as presidents," wishing to remain in a subordinate post, *TNP*, p. 451,452.

Chapter 17: "...we will esteem learning and discipline..." *TAS*, p.284

1. letter: November 6, 1828 Indiana University Archives. (letter footnote indicates 1825 start) and letter of July 4, 1838.

2. Dr. Maxwell quote: Thomas D. Clark, *Indiana University, Midwest Pioneer*, p. 39.

3. steamboat: *TNP*, p. 479.

4. new president: *ibid.*, pp. 451–452, 463, 486–496 are pages devoted to "Dr. Bloduplex," the fictitious name for Andrew Wylie. Also see Guide to IU President's Office records 28-52, and "no more than ushers," *TNP*, p. 490. Pages 477 to 496 are omitted in the 1855 revised edition.

5. Borland-Hall deed: Monroe County Deed Records, Book B, p. 203. James Borland was responsible for the entire seminary square survey.

6. first graduates: James Dunn, James Rollins, Michael Hummer, William Hamilton Stockwell; see IU histories. Most have biography online. Rollins called "Father of the University of Missouri," was Missouri governor. *The Indianapolis Sunday Star*, May 18, 1941 states: Findley Dodds, James F. Dodds, Aaron Ferguson, Hamilton Stockwell, John Todd, Michael Hummer,

Samuel C. Dunn, James W. Dunn, James A. Maxwell, Jr., and Joseph A. Wright (and later William McKee Dunn) were first students. James F. Dodds is James Findley (or Finley) Dodds. The three Dunns named are brothers and nephews of Dr. Maxwell. I believe Findley Dodds is Samuel Fin(d)ley Dodds, Jr. and it can be supposed the name is in honor of Rev. Samuel Finley, a College of New Jersey president and Hall-connected relative of Dr. Benjamin Rush. Also see "Charge to the IUPUI Class of 2003," http://www.homepages.indiana.edu/053003/text/viewpoint.html, Gerald L. Bepko, Interim Indiana University President, speech; and David Banta's Foundation Day Addresses, making up first six Chapters of James A. Woodburn's *History of Indiana University*, Vol. 1.

7. "Some will think we are manufacturing a character..." *TNP*, p. 488.

8. Hall-Wylie: See notes above.

9. Henodelphisterian Society: Indiana University Athenian Society. Records of the Athenian Society, 1830–1886. Collection 135; http://www.indiana.educ/~libarch/Inst/135inst.html.

10. James Dunn: "George," *TNP*, p. 425, 426, and letter to Nunemacher, August 14, 1855.

11. Joseph A. Wright: "Henry," *TNP*, p.426–428; *ibid.*

12. IR: autobiography, family records.

13. deed to Vance Jones: Monroe County Deed Records, Book C, p. 329.

14. anonymous letter, *TNP*, p. 490.

15. Andrew Wylie, Jr. 1882 letter to Banta: Collection 203, Wylie Family, Folder 1, Correspondence, Indiana University Archives, Bloomington.

16. Banta, David D.: Dr. Banta's addresses.

Chapter 18: "...how our faculty spent vacations in the woods." *TNP*, p.428

1. in the woods: *ibid.*, p. 428–429.

2. cave expedition: *ibid.*, p. 428–440.

3. hunting passenger pigeons: *ibid.*, p.466–473.

4. Austin Seward is briefly mentioned in my work, but he was a cherished friend of BRH; an entire chapter is devoted to him, *ibid.*, p. 277–286. Seward's character can be discerned from BRH's sobriquet for him: *Vulcanus Allheart.*

Chapter 19: "...a mind taught by many sorrows..." *TNP*, p. 477.

1. exhibition: *ibid.*, p. 502; see also Clark's *Indiana University*, chapter "Laying the

Bottom Rail," p. 25–48. Also see *TNP*, p. 415–424.

2. knife incident: *TNP*, p. 508.

3. scarlet fever; Elizabeth dies: IR: *The Youth's Book; TNP*, p.475–477. Extensive search found no record of where the child's body was buried.

4. "…he resigned and for weeks past had been preparing to leave the Purchase." *TNP*, p.517.

5. Harney and Wylie on the boardwalk: *ibid.*, p. 414.

6. faculty wars: These episodes are told often in Indiana University histories, articles, to the point of overkill. In *TNP*, pp. 414, 502–518, as well as pages already listed.

7. BRH sells to Harney: Monroe County Deed Records, Book D, p. 62.

8. IR: autobiography.

9. See earlier Harney references. Also *TNP*, p. 518.

10. Halls leave, *ibid.*, p. 519–522.

Chapter 20: "...there are no *accidents*..." *SFE*, p.191

1. Hall to Bedford: Schell, William P., *The Annals of Bedford County, Pennsylvania*, Gazette Publishing Company—condensed

sketches, prepared for Old Home Week August 4–10, 1907; Bedford County Historical Society. Also see Martha Doughty Reed letters from Bedford Springs. All of Martha's letters: pages 88 to 132 in *The Youth's Book*. Letter to Barclay from BRH, March 13, 1838, Samuel M. Barclay Papers, Harvard Law School Library, Box No. 1, folder 1-25, 1838.

2. history of the Bedford Presbyterian Church: including notes, sketches and lecture by pastor Robert F. Sample, from Bedford County, Pennsylvania Historical Society Pioneer Library.

3. Bedford Academy Brochure: dated July 7, 1835, text from copy from American Antiquarian Society, 185 Salisbury St., Worcester, Massachusetts.

4 IR: autobiography.

5. Martha Doughty letter: Worthington B. Williams Family Papers, Indiana Historical Society, William H. Smith Memorial Library.

6. "We prefer an admixture of various and opposite studies," *TAS*, p. 131.

7. Mann, Duane, Thompson, Reeside, Potter, Huidekoper: biographies online.

8. Martha Doughty Reed letters: March 6, 1835; July 8, 1837; *The Youth's Book*.

9. Latin Grammar: My copy is a 4-inch by 7-inch book, 140 pages, exactly 1/2-inch thick. The title is almost bigger than the book. Publisher Harrison Hall was a brother of John E. Hall and James Hall; their mother wrote an early history of Philadelphia. (Sharf and Westcott's *History of Philadelphia* 1609–1884, L.H. Everts & Co.) Not believed to be related to BRH.

10. Baynard Chisholm Hall dies: *The Bedford Gazette*, October 26, 1833.

11. Selby Harney: From Robert Sample documents. Although Sample says their graves were enclosed by a fence, when we visited the cemetery all stones had been rearranged in orderly rows. No grave markers could be found for Harney and the Hall child.

Chapter 21: "A school is sometimes called the world in miniature." *TAS*, p. 25

1. IR, autobiography; Martha Doughty Reed letters, *The Youth's Book;* Worthington B. Williams Family Papers.

2. escape of John Holliday: printed in *The Bedford Gazette*, September 29, 1837, Bedford, Pennsylvania, and then in book form, 15 pages. Copies in William L. Clements Library, University of Michigan, Ann Arbor, and Yale University Library, New Haven, Connecticut.

3. Samuel Barclay letter, see Chapter 20, note 1.

4. *Disciplined Youth:* Printed by I. Ashmead & Company of Philadelphia in 1838 as a booklet of 16 pages. I own an original.

5. "...teaching is a holy vocation." in *TAS*, p. 37.

6. teacher as artist: *ibid.*, pp.18,19, 21.

7. literary review: *The Literary and Theological Review*, Appleton, 1839, Chapter 5.

8. lecture at Spring-Villa in Bordentown, New Jersey, printed by Powell & George, Printers, August 1839; the lecture is in praise of educated women.

9. land grant sold: See Chapter 1, note 10.

10. honorary degree: Records from Seeley Mudd Library, Princeton University, and Princeton Theological Seminary.

11. "imperishable classic" from Dr. James Woodburn, introduction to 1916 Princeton edition of *TNP.*

12. Williams family: Reed family records, also Worthington B. Williams Family Papers: BRH letter, February 20, 1855.

13. Bartlett's school: BRH letter, June 3, 1847; Worthington B. Williams Family Papers; Smith, James H., *History of Dutchess County, New York*, p. 407, 408.

14. "rewards and punishments," from reference to James Roosevelt in Cushman papers, Yale Library; letters of Edward, George, James Cushman while attending Bartlett's school.

15. Roosevelt: from *Before the Trumpet: Young Franklin Roosevelt 1882-1905*, Geoffrey C. Ward, Harper & Rowe, New York, 1985, and Cushman letters.

16. John Holmes death: John Finley Crowe's record of admissions and dismissals, Hanover Presbyterian Church, Hanover College Archives.

Chapter 22: "I have long discerned the hands of a gracious Providence..." *SFE*, p.105.

1. "every elevation..." in Preface to *Something for Every Body*...

2. Dutchess Academy: Board minutes from Adriance Memorial Library, Poughkeepsie, New York. *History of Dutchess County.*

3. BRH letter to Worthington Williams, June 1, 1847; Worthington B. Williams Family Papers.

4. Newburgh, Orange County: Principals, http://www.rootsweb.com/~nyorange/nfa.htm;

5. Rev. Alexander: Review in *The Biblical Repertory and Princeton Review*, Vol. 20, No. 1, 1848.

6. Rutgers degree: Rutgers Special Collections and University Archives, Mudd Library, Princeton; Union College questionnaire. Curious typed note, undated, in Rutgers files, by a C. A. Watson who asks, "For Rutgers it would be interesting to know just why he was worthy og thr [sic] honorable degree."

7. James W. Alexander, *Forty Years of Familiar Letters of James Waddell Alexander,* 1860.

8. "every reason to love his profession.," *TAS,* Preface xi. Also see p. 21, 37.

9. family news: letter to Worthington Williams, June 1, 1847, Williams Family Papers.

10. "last book," the 900 copies refers to *Something for Every Body…*

Chapter 23: "What an evil is the system." *FF,* p. 45

1. BRH knew at least three former slave-holders in Indiana (although not plantation owners): Ephraim Goss, Dr. Maxwell and Williamson Dunn, all Kentucky residents before coming to Indiana.

2. *New York Evangelist:* December 9, 1852, unsigned.

3. *New York Observer:* December 9, 1852, unsigned.

4. *Godey's Ladys Book*, February 1853, Philadelphia. p.178.

5. Pyrnelle: *Diddie, Dumps and Tot or Plantation Child-Life*, Louise-Clarke Pyrnelle, Harper Brothers, New York, 1910, Preface.

6. the slave-dealer: *FF*, p.85.

7. "May God dispose..." in *FF*, p. 239.

8. Reeds separated by miles: Reed autobiography.

9. *Prodessi Quam Conspici:* Scribner printed; phrase is motto of Miami University, Oxford, Ohio. *Trenton Gazette*, June 30, 1852. See Chapter 3, note 2.

10. Elinor Reed letter to IR: Worthington Williams Family Papers, December 29, 1850, "on the farm."

Chapter 24: "...every noble thing demands a sacrifice." *FF*, p.278.

1. Beecher: Beecher's sermons and printed works are prolific; see Ward & Trent, et al., *The Cambridge History of English and American Literature*, New York; Bartleby. com, 2000 (www.bartleby.com/cambridge). I drew from many sources for the opinions of HWB.

2. Park Institute: The last home of the Halls may not have been the original Park

Institute; owners of the home believe an
earlier building on the same street was the
original. If so, then it is probably another
move indicating a further economic
downslide for the Halls.

3. creek: It is possible that the creek near the
   house was a source of typhoid fever owing
   to the poor sanitation of the time.

4. Rush's death notice: *The New York Times,*
   March 14, 1854.

5. symptoms in *FF,* p.116.

6. Mrs. Henry Ward (Eunice) Beecher: *From
   Dawn to Daylight: or the Simple Story of a
   Western Home,* p. 212.

7. Dr. David Maxwell died May 24, 1854, at
   the home of his son, Dr. James Darwin
   Maxwell, in Bloomington.

Chapter 25: "I am ready—whenever you say I may
begin." BRH letter to Nunemacher, August 27,
1855.

1. Nunemacher letters: Letters from BRH
   to John Nunemacher in New Albany;
   February 20, 1855, to condense into one
   volume. Nunemacher had published James
   Abbey's *California, A Trip Across the Plains
   in the Spring of 1850,* the travel genre
   becoming popular.

2. letters: August 27, 1855; new title, from

*The New Purchase: or Seven and a Half
Years in the Far West* to *The New Purchase
or, Early Years in the Far West.* The pen
name, Robert Carlton, Esq. remained, *ibid.*

3. Jacob Lowe reference: *ibid.*

4. Wylie references: April 18 letter and "key"
    letter, undated.

5. libel law: letter, August 14, 1855.

6. Momberger: biographical material online;
    letter September 9, 1855.

7. phiz: diminutive for physiognomy.

8. illustrations: Nunemacher letters; August
    27, September 20, October 6, 19, 1855.

9. "....my life for about 8 years," in letter
    with key to names, undated, Nunemacher
    papers.

10. Whitman's *Leaves of Grass:* http://
    www.poets.org/poets/poets.
    cfm?45332B7C000C0707E, The Academy
    of American Poets, 1997–2004.

11. William McCalla: letter, August 14, 1855,
    Nunemacher papers. Bush and McClean:
    undated letter, *ibid.*

12. Dr. Maxwell, Seward, James Maxwell:
    letter, *ibid.* Also October 6.

13. Dr. Davidson: undated letter, Nunemacher
    papers.

14. Kirkland: Mentioned as authoress of "The New Home," letter, February 20, 1855, Nunemacher papers. Interestingly, Kirkland and Hall's lifespans covered the same years.

15. Seward complimentary copy: undated key letter, *ibid.*

16. Dr. Cheever: letter, December 21, 1855, *ibid.*

17. James Brewer: letter, December 19, 1855, *ibid.*

18. "book appears to be dead" in letter, July 12, 1856, *ibid.*

19. "bitter defense of Romanism," *ibid.*

Chapter 26: "An honorable scar or two..." in Spring-Villa Seminary address, p. 8

1. letter: Worthington Williams Family Papers, September 29, 1857.

2. Bordentown: history at http://www.nynjctbotany.org/njiptofc/bordentowntwn.htm

3. Josiah Williams, letters to father: Worthington Williams Family Papers, March 1, October 10, 1857.

4. Hall to Worthington Williams, letter, September 29, 1857, Williams Family Papers.

5. Isaac Reed: Williams Papers, Reed family records, Hanford A. Edson, p. 115. *Olney Times,* Olney, Illinois, February 19, 1858. Gravestone in Olney Cemetery.

Chapter 27: "Stream nearly run out." Union College Questionnaire.

1. Brasier: Blanchard, *History of Owen County,* p. 701. Owen Deed Record Book 1, (homesteaders); *TNP,* p.134, 135. BRH gives him the name Ashford, identifies him as Mr. Brasier in letter to Nunemacher August 14, 1855.

2. Amorphites: as in "amorphous."

3. "Esau and Jacob," ironically a biblical account of deceit and an inheritance; *SFE,* p. 114. Hall's interest in theater would have included playwriting.

4. tool-books: *ibid.,* p. 115.

5. See legal opinion of 1795 land grant quiet title, Chapter 1, and Chapter 1 note 10.

6. years of darkness, *SFE,* p.108–110.

7. Edistina Hall death: *Brooklyn Eagle,* May 24, 1859. Cemetery of the Evergreens, Brooklyn, Kings County, New York.

8. 1860 census: Brooklyn, Kings County, New York.

9. REVERIE: On my way to Indianapolis: *TNP,* p. 213, 214, 1855 edition.

10. All in one cabin: *TNP,* p. 89.

11. Yes, I do steal off: *ibid.,* p.105.

Chapter 28: "Words are Things" speech, *The New York Times,* December 4, 1858.

l. George W. Reed: Josiah Williams in the Union Army wrote letters home during his service; related the details of his uncle's death; Worthington Williams papers. Civil War battles involving the cousins, see Epilogue note 2.

2. Hall obituary: *Brooklyn Eagle,* January 24, 1863; *New York Times,* January 27, 1863. John Rousmaniere in his (2008) *Green Oasis in Brooklyn: The Evergreens Cemetery 1849-2008* states that BRH taught poor black children in Brooklyn.

3. death certificate: New York City Dept. of Records and Information Services, Municipal Archives, 31 Chambers Street, New York. Cemetery of the Evergreens, Brooklyn.

4. Rev. Sample lecture at Bedford, Pennsylvania

5. Carolina Hall: Death certificate, New York City Dept. of Records and Information Services, above. *Brooklyn Eagle,* February 2, 1864. Cemetery of the Evergreens, Brooklyn.

6. Aunt Doughty: Martha Holme Doughty, gravestone, Cemetery of the Evergreens.

7. Mary Ann Young Hall: Affidavit of Alex Wilson, cousin, in Kings County Surrogates Court; probate of Mary Ann Hall Will, November 12, 1864. Cemetery of the Evergreens. This may be the same Alexander C. Wilson, journalist and lawyer, born in Trenton, 1824, living in New York during his career as a writer. See mention in Chapter 25.

8. Martha Morris Young: Affidavit of Sarah M. F. Scott, Kings County Surrogate Court, November 20, 1866; probate of Martha Morris Young Will. Cemetery of the Evergreens.

Epilogue

1. letter from Martha Morris Young to sister Elinor Reed, Worthington Williams Papers.

2. the relatives serving in the Civil War: See *Gallant Fourteenth: The Story of an Indiana Civil War Regiment,* Nancy Niblack Baxter, Pioneer Study Center Press, 1980; *The Iron Brigade: A Military History,* Alan T. Nolan, Indiana University Press edition, 1994; and *Giants in the Cornfield,* Wilbur D. Jones, White Mane Publishing, 1997.

3. Will of Mary Ann Hall: Kings County Surrogate Court records, New York.

4. Will of Martha M. Young; Kings County Surrogate Court records.

5. George W. Reed's memorial gravestone in Olney Cemetery, Olney, Illinois. Josiah Williams letters.

6. Elinor Reed: Reed family records; Williams-Reed Cemetery, Putnam County, Indiana.

7. Sarah and William Shackleford: Reed family records; 1860 Clarksville, Tennessee census; see also George Washington portrait by Oliver Frazer and William S. Shackleford: http//www.lrc.ky.gov/kidspages/images/photo13.gif

8. John Morris Young: Newton County, Missouri census, 1870.

9. Sarah M. F. Scott: Will of Martha Morris Young above, see land grant, Chapter 1, in note10. Wedding: *New York Times,* May 16, 1867. Sarah's father John was an army officer. She may have been both a student and a teacher associated with Halls and perhaps their connection was made when the Halls were in Newburgh, New York near West Point.

10. "Proceedings of the Southwestern Indiana Historical Society," Evansville, published by Indiana Historical Commission,

Indianapolis, Bulletin No. 18, October
1923, p. 68–70.

Dramatis Personae "Expressed or Implied"

Adams, John
Allen, Mr.
Allen, William G.
Allison
Allison, James Montgomery Higgins
Alexander, Rev. James W.
Anderson, Walter
Appleton, publisher
Armstrong, Rev. William
Arnold, Ben
Ashbrook, Thomas
Ashers
Asher, Bartlett
Asher, Susan
Ashford
Ashmore

Banta, David
Banta, R. E.
Banta, Richard
Barclay, Samuel M.
Bartlett, Charles
Batterton, Matilda (Maxwell)
Batterton, Peter
Baynard, Ephraim
Baynard Elizabeth Ann (Hall)
Baynard Elizabeth (Grimball)

Clarence, Charles
Clapp, Dr. Ashbel
Clay, Henry
Compher, John S.
Conner, John
Conner, William
Conway, Peter
Cooper, James Fenimore
Cradock, John
Crockett, Davy
Crowe, Rev. John Finley
Cumpher, Mr.
Cushman, Edward
Cushman, George
Cushman, James
Cutswell, "Insidias"
Cutswell, William

Davidson, Rev. Robert
Daviess, Joseph
Dickey, Rev. J. M.
Dodds, Findley
Dodds, James F.
Doughty, Aunt
Doughty, Martha (Holmes)
Doughty, Robert Jr.
Doughty, Thomas T.
Doughty, William
Drayton, Glen
Duane, William J.

Dunagan, Solomon
Dunn, James
Dunn, James Wilson
Dunn, Mary
Dunn, Samuel Campbell
Dunn, William McKee
Dunn, Williamson
Dunning, Paris
Durkee, Charille

Eckles, Elizabeth
Eliot, Mrs.
Elliott, Elizabeth Ann
Elliott, Thomas
Elssler, Fannie
Etty
Evans, Christmas

Ferguson, Aaron
Forster, Mr.
Freeland
Freeland, Benjamin
Fuller, Ben

Gentry, Allen
Gentry, James
George III
Girard, Stephen
Girault, Arsene Napoleon
Goss, Ephraim

Goss, Joseph
Green, Duff
Grimball, Elizabeth
Grimball, Paul
Grimball, William
Gunn, Senator James

Hadden, Joseph
Hall, Baynard Chisholm
Hall, Baynard Rush
Hall, Carolina Baynard
Hall, Elisha
Hall, Dr. Elisha
Hall, Edistina Morris
Hall, Elizabeth Ann (Baynard)
Hall, Elizabeth (niece)
Hall, Elizabeth (daughter)
Hall, Harrison
Hall, Holmes Baynard
Hall, James
Hall, Dr. John
Hall, John (infant)
Hall, John E.
Hall, Joseph
Hall, Mary Ann (Young)
Hall, Richard
Hall, Rush Baynard
Hall, Ruth (Hall)
Ham, Rev. Mizraim
Hamilton, Alexander

Morgan, Ben M.
Morgan, Dr. Samuel
Morris, Robert
Mundy, Bridget

Napoleon
Nelson, Rev. Samuel Kelsey
Nicholson, Meredith
Nott, Eliphalet
Nunemacher, John

Otto, J. C.

Paine, Tom (Thomas)
Payne
Payne, Dolley (Todd, Madison)
Payne, William
Parks, Mrs.
Parsons, Rev. William
Penn, John
Penn, Thomas
Penn, William
Perren, Mrs.
Peterson, Daphne
Pillbox, Dr.
Pinter, Harold
Poe, Edgar Allen
Potter, Elderkin
Pratt, Henry
Pyrnelle, Louise Clark

Wallace, Aletha
Wallace, Lew
Wallace, Margaret
Wallace, Martha Rankin
Wallace, Mrs.
Wallace, William Ross
Walter, Richard
Washington, George
Washington, Martha
Watson, C. A.
Webster, Noah
Welden
Whitcomb, James
White Andy
Whitman, George
Whitman, Walt
Whitman, Walter
Williams, Julia Edistina
Williams, Josiah (elder)
Williams, Josiah
Williams, Lydia (Reed)
Williams, Worthington
Wilmar, Colonel
Wilson, Alex
Wilson, Alexander
Woodburn, Dr. James Albert
Woodward, W. E.
Wright, Joseph Albert
Wyatt, John
Wylie, Andrew Jr.

Wylie, Andrew Sr.

Young, Aletha (Wallace)
Young, Ann (Holmes)
Young, Elinor (Reed)
Young, John Morris Jr.
Young, John Morris Sr.
Young, Martha Morris (Miss Emily)
Young, Mary Ann (Hall)
Young, Nicholas Jr.
Young, Nicholas Sr.
Young, Wallace H.